Index on Censorship

Free Word Centre, 60 Farringdon Road, London, ECIR 3GA

Chief Executive John Kampfner **Editor** Jo Glanville **Associate Editor** Rohan Jayasekera **Assistant Editor** Natasha Schmidt **News Editor** Padraig Reidy **Online Editor** Emily Butselaar **Head of Arts & Events** Julia Farrington **Finance Manager** David Sewell **Curator** Klara Chlupata **Public Affairs Manager** Michael Harris **Fundraising Coordinator** Lizzie Rusbridger **Sub-editor** Caroline Palmer **Interns and Editorial Assistants** Ángel García Català, Ed Gillett, Angel Ko, David Paton, Michael Riordan, Eleonora Vio, Pete Ward, Kathie Wu, John Young
Graphic designer Sam Hails
Cover design Brett Biedscheid
Printed by Page Bros., Norwich, UK

Volume 39 No 3 2010

If you are interested in republishing any article featured in this issue, please contact us at permissions@indexoncensorship.org

Supported by
ARTS COUNCIL ENGLAND

MUSIC AND SILENCE

Jo Glanville

'Music is so powerful because it is a physical expression of the human soul,' says Daniel Barenboim in an exclusive interview for *Index*. 'It attacks, I would say, all the functions of the human being – the brain, the heart, the stomach, the temperament. That's what makes it so dangerous. Music is *much* more powerful than words.' Barenboim famously made a stand when he defied Israel's ban on performing Wagner; his celebrated West-Eastern Divan orchestra transcends the political separation that divides the Middle East.

All the musicians who have written and given interviews for this special issue on music and censorship are remarkable for their courage and commitment. Some live in countries where artistic expression can be interpreted as an act of protest. As a collective art form that brings people together in its execution and performance, musicians and their audience can be especially vulnerable. In Burma, Tibet and Iran, musicians and their fans are forced underground: Ayatollah Khamenei recently reinforced the censorship of musicians in Iran when he announced this summer that music was 'not compatible' with the values of the Islamic Republic. In this issue, Negar Shaghaghi gives a vivid account of smuggling rock music home as a schoolgirl in Tehran; Femi Kuti, one of world music's most celebrated stars, has to endure repeated intimidation from the government in Nigeria; Kurdish singer Ferhat Tunç is currently facing prosecution in Turkey for making a political statement at a concert; Lapiro de Mbanga is serving a prison sentence in Cameroon, in harsh conditions, charged with inciting violence.

But censorship of music and musicians doesn't necessarily take such extreme forms. As Peter Jenner, veteran manager of Pink Floyd, Tyrannosaurus Rex, The Clash and other legendary bands, points out, the whole music industry is predicated on censorship. There is a subtle process of selection that filters out music that challenges the norm, in which the media and the music business collude. Khyam Allami's investigation of the independent music scene in the Middle East highlights this trend. The

digital revolution has posed the most significant challenge to the old order (as well as liberating access to music in authoritarian regimes). Radiohead's Colin Greenwood writes about his band's decision to release their last album digitally and escape the confines of traditional distribution.

This is the first issue of Index dedicated to music in more than a decade ('Smashed Hits' 6/98) and we're delighted once again to be producing this edition in association with Marie Korpe and Ole Reitov of Freemuse. As the only organisation committed to supporting musicians who face censorship, Freemuse has been an outstanding champion of freedom of expression. Their article is a sobering account of the silencing of musical expression over the past 30 years. It includes a gripping description of the tactics used by the secret police in South Africa to destroy the career of musician Roger Lucey during the apartheid years. It's a chilling reminder of the lengths that regimes will go to in seeking to control and silence free expression, in all its forms.

You can listen to a selection of some of the music chosen by our writers for this issue on Spotify and iTunes (www.indexoncensorship.org/music). We're also delighted to include Chaza Charafeddine's glorious portraits – in colour – from her new exhibition in Beirut. As always, you can follow daily censorship stories on our website www.indexoncensorship.org ❒

©Jo Glanville
39(3): 1/5
DOI: 10.1177/0306422010381549
www.indexoncensorship.org

CONTENTS

DIVINE COMEDY

BRING MUSIC, BRING LIFE

Daniel Barenboim tells Clemency Burton-Hill why music provides a model for living and governments continue to fear the power of its influence

In 2001, the celebrated pianist and conductor Daniel Barenboim was accused of 'cultural rape' and branded a 'fascist' in Israel for conducting the work of Richard Wagner as the second encore during a concert in Jerusalem. A 40-minute chat with the audience had preceded the performance of the piece – the Prelude and Liebestod from *Tristan und Isolde* – during which time Barenboim had asked if the audience would like to hear it, and invited anyone who felt uncomfortable to leave. Around 2 per cent of the audience left; those who remained gave Barenboim and his orchestra, the Berlin Staatskapelle, a standing ovation. Wagner's music has been censored, unofficially, in Israel since 1938.

In recent years, Barenboim has become increasingly vocal on non-musical issues, especially the Arab-Israeli conflict. He holds Israeli citizenship. In 1999, together with his close friend, the late Palestinian academic Edward Said, Barenboim founded the West-Eastern Divan Orchestra, an ensemble of more than 120 young musicians who hail from the Middle East – Israel, Palestine, Lebanon, Syria, Jordan – and other Muslim countries including Egypt, Iran and Turkey. Each summer, the orchestra comes together in Seville, where its

Daniel Barenboim conducts the Vienna Philharmonic Orchestra
New Year's Concert, 2009
Credit: Herwig Prammer/Reuters

members are issued with Spanish diplomatic passports allowing them freedom of movement, before launching an international tour. The orchestra is not able to perform in most of the countries represented by its members, but has enjoyed phenomenal critical acclaim elsewhere in the world.

Barenboim was born in Argentina in 1942 to Russian-Jewish parents. He gave his first piano recital in Buenos Aires aged just seven, moved with his family to Israel aged ten, and was being described by conductor Wilhelm Furtwängler as a 'phenomenon' by the time he was 11. The former music director of the Chicago Symphony Orchestra, Barenboim was named Conductor for Life at the Berlin Staatsoper in 2000 and Maestro Scaligero at La Scala, Milan, in 2006. The recipient of numerous awards for his conducting, piano recordings and human rights work, he is also the author of three books: A Life In Music, Parallels and Paradoxes (with Edward W Said), and Everything Is Connected, in which he outlines his belief that music offers us a unique model for understanding human relations and the world.

Clemency Burton-Hill, the granddaughter of a Jew from Belarus, is a British writer, broadcaster and violinist who has been involved with music projects in the West Bank and occupied Palestinian territories since 2004, including the al Kamandjati refugee camp music schools in Ramallah and Jenin. In January 2009, she was invited by Daniel Barenboim to join the West-Eastern Divan Orchestra as an honorary violinist on their tenth anniversary tour. She has also interviewed Barenboim on a number of occasions in print and on television, including the Proms, the BBC's Culture Show, and the Berlin Philharmonic's 2010 Europa Konzert, which will be broadcast on BBC4 later this year.

Clemency Burton-Hill: One of my strongest memories of rehearsing with you and the West-Eastern Divan is a moment when you reminded the members of the orchestra that every single one of their governments would stop them from being there if they could, and that what they were doing was therefore very brave. For all the adulation and acclaim that the Divan garners around the world, it strikes me that it is, essentially, a censored orchestra.

Daniel Barenboim: Yes, you're probably right. The Divan is not acceptable to any of the countries represented by its members. We can't play in any Arab countries except the Emirates, nor in Israel. The Israelis don't understand why it is even necessary to make the gesture. And the Arab world mostly sees the Divan as a way of normalisation, in the sense of accepting Israel, and all the problems that involves.

Clemency Burton-Hill: So the fact that those kids come together to make music with each other every year, in the face of governments who would silence them and despite recriminations from their friends and family at home, feels like something of a defiant act.

Daniel Barenboim: It is. And you know, I believe more and more that it is up to individuals – or minorities – to express things which are not acceptable to the majority. Because there is always a special angle that an individual or a minority can have. And maybe the majority will eventually follow, but you cannot start a new idea that is going to change things with the blessing of the majority.

Clemency Burton-Hill: How important is it that the orchestra be allowed to make music freely in the Middle East?

Daniel Barenboim: I think the full dimensions of the Divan will only be achieved when we are able to play in Tel Aviv, Damascus, Beirut, Cairo, because that is really what it is all about. On the other hand, if the conflict was resolved there would hardly be a need for the Divan. And so it is a bit of a contradiction in terms. The Divan came into existence and continues to develop because of the conflict, and it has not yet been fully able to push through its idea of accepting the narrative of the other, the point of view of the other. For that you need a yearning voice for justice and for compassion, from both sides. And the Israelis as a majority I don't think have a compassion for the rights of the Palestinians, otherwise they wouldn't be occupying the territories for so many years and they wouldn't blockade Gaza.

Clemency Burton-Hill: You have said that 'Our challenge in the 21st century is to use music not only as an escape from life – in the sense that you come home fed up, put on music, and forget your troubles – but also as a way of making sense of the world. Music is not an alternative to living; it's a model for living.' So when music is censored, or silenced, is there much more at stake than merely entertainment and pleasure?

Daniel Barenboim: Yes, of course. I think history has shown us that many people are afraid of the effect of music. It can be very exalting, it brings people to expressions of solidarity and of enthusiasm – which is not always the case with the government. That is why music was used and manipulated so unashamedly by dictatorships. By the Nazis, by the Soviets ...

Clemency Burton-Hill: And, ironically, those governments that manipulate music for their own purposes are often the states that censor it most cynically.

Daniel Barenboim: Because music is very powerful. It is very difficult to remain unmoved by music, I think probably for the simple fact that it has a physical penetration through the ear, which is much stronger than through the eye. If I don't like what I am seeing, I can close my eyes. But if I don't like what I am hearing, I cannot close my ears; I mean, I can, artificially, I can put my fingers in my ears, but basically there is a penetration, a physical penetration, which makes it very powerful indeed.

Clemency Burton-Hill: I have heard you say there is something 'subversive' about music.

Daniel Barenboim: Edward Said always used to say that music is subversive. When you have a beautiful melody played by a woodwind instrument, very often the accompaniment, say, in the strings, will subvert that. Yet at the same time, the full expression of the line will be totally dependent on it too. There are many, many lessons to be learned from that.

Clemency Burton-Hill: Is it possible to describe why music is so powerful, why it acts on us the way it does?

Daniel Barenboim: Well, I think music is so powerful because it is, first of all, a physical thing, a physical expression of the human soul; something that is not only in the thought. And it attacks, I would say, all the functions of the human being. It attacks the brain, and it attacks the heart, and it attacks the stomach, you know, the temperament. Each one of us reacts perhaps with one more than any other of those three elements, but all three are constantly in action, and that's what makes it so dangerous. Music is much more powerful than words.

Clemency Burton-Hill: Which is why censorship of music has always existed, and still exists?

Daniel Barenboim: Yes. By the way, there is a wonderful book called Beethoven in German Politics [by David B. Dennis]. It documents how Bismarck, Hitler, and then in the East German Republic, how Beethoven was used for their purposes, and how Hitler managed to convince the world that Beethoven's Ninth was the perfect example of German spirituality with a text that says 'all men are brothers – except a few', namely the Jews.

Clemency Burton-Hill: That brings us to an important point about the de facto censorship of Wagner in Israel. You have always been adamant that Wagner was originally banned after Kristallnacht in 1938 not because of his own anti-Semitism – which had been well known since the 19th century – but because of the anti-Semitism of the Nazi party, i.e. the monstrous and appalling uses to which Hitler put the music. That distinction seems still not to be being made in Israel today, where the ban is very much still in place.

Daniel Barenboim: I'm afraid Israeli public opinion has manipulated all that. I'm sure there are many people in Israel who 'don't want to hear Wagner' who think that Wagner was around in 1940 – that Wagner was a Nazi. But you know, none other than [Arturo] Toscanini – who besides being a great musician was a great fighter for liberty – in 1936, when he was conducting the opening concerts for the new symphony orchestra in Tel Aviv, ironically then called the Palestine Philharmonic, played Wagner and there was no problem. The decision to stop playing Wagner was taken by members of the orchestra after Kristallnacht and that was perfectly understandable and just, from my point of view, in 1938. But to continue with that now is arguably as bad as it would have been to continue to play Wagner from that day.

Clemency Burton-Hill: It seems ironic that you were accused of being a fascist for playing Wagner's music, when it could be argued that censorship of any music in a democratic country is verging on the fascist.

Daniel Barenboim: As I have said before, the idea this was a scandal was started the following day by people with a political agenda, not those in the concert hall, which greatly saddened me. I have always said that I respect anybody's right not to listen to Wagner and that is why his work should be offered to a non-subscription audience. Israel is a democratic society, there should be no place for such taboos.

Clemency Burton-Hill: Have you ever had any problems from members of the West-Eastern Divan who perhaps did not want to play Wagner?

Daniel Barenboim: No, in fact it was the Israeli members who asked me to play Wagner in the first place, in 2004 or 2005. It was the brass players, who came and asked me to programme some Wagner because they couldn't play it in Israel, they could not hear it in Israel, but they felt that musically it was very important to them, and they had no problem with it.

Clemency Burton-Hill: How depressing is it, to you, that it is now almost a decade since you played that Wagner encore in Jerusalem, and yet the debate about whether his music should still be banned from live performance seems not to have moved forward at all – rather backwards?

Daniel Barenboim: Yes, but the whole of Israeli society, from my point of view, has humanly moved backwards over those ten years.

Clemency Burton-Hill: You have made an explicit connection between this issue and Israel's relationship with the Palestinians and the conflict today, suggesting that the Wagner ban means Israelis have not yet made the transition into being Israeli Jews and are still identifying themselves with the Judaism of the 30s and 40s. You have said: 'Until we are able to do that, we will not be able to establish a fruitful dialogue with non-Jews' and pointed out that while a sense of history is imperative, Israel must also look forward.

Daniel Barenboim: Yes, well, it is the same instinct that would allow so many Israelis to deny the Palestinians who live in Israel, the so-called Israeli Arabs, their human rights; to not allow civil marriages; the same instinct that means there is no separation of the synagogue and government, which is something that is accepted in most of the world. The other place where it is not accepted is Iran!

Clemency Burton-Hill: Talking about Iran, the authorities there have banned all teaching of all musical instruments in all schools because 'the use of musical instruments is against the principles of our value system', according to Education Minister Ali Bagherzadeh. Any school in Iran that teaches music may now be permanently closed and its director barred. What do you think of that?

Daniel Barenboim: Well, one has to say that music has not played the role in the Muslim world that it has played in Europe for centuries, so in a way they are sadly more ignorant about the nature of what music is. For them, music is something to celebrate with at weddings and mourn with at funerals, but they don't view it as an expression of the human quality of life. They don't understand that when you play a piece of music, whether it is a Chopin Nocturne or a huge Bruckner Symphony, that this is the story of human life, it tells us something of the quality of humanity. This is what makes us moved when we listen to music.

Clemency Burton-Hill: The West-Eastern Divan contains some young Iranian musicians within its ranks. How do you find their attitudes?

Daniel Barenboim: Those youngsters obviously do not share the opinions of their government about the nature of music. As you know, they are wonderful musicians, they have a huge capacity of giving, of generosity.

Clemency Burton-Hill: And I don't think it's too idealistic to suggest that their experiences making music, especially in the West-Eastern Divan, have probably nourished and developed that capacity. The orchestra is what brings them together with Israelis and Arabs, but music leads these youngsters to all sorts of other connections – they talk about politics, football, pop music, films; they fall in and out of love with each other; they begin to understand and accept the narrative of the other and take what they have learned back home. Isn't it a tragedy that young Iranians will henceforth be denied the right to even learn a musical instrument? To my mind that's a particularly pernicious form of music censorship; silencing it before it even exists!

Daniel Barenboim: In the end, though, when people forbid things, it is because they are afraid of them. It is not a sign of strength, it is a sign of weakness.

Clemency Burton-Hill: Yes – I have been struck by that often, travelling through the occupied territories with musicians. I have watched Israeli soldiers turn away young Palestinian musicians and singers at checkpoints as if somehow playing Bach or singing Puccini were a genuine threat to the state of Israel. And it always smacks of such monumental cowardice, even if the soldier is wielding a gun. Especially when the soldier is wielding a gun.

Daniel Barenboim: Exactly.

Clemency Burton-Hill: And whoever it was who burned down the al Kamandjati music centre in Jenin, or destroyed the Gaza music school; such acts feel like a despicable yet rather pathetic attempt to silence the

Palestinian's fledgling right to express themselves, through music, as a people. As Ramzi Aburedwan [founder of the al Kamandjati music school and viola player in the West-Eastern Divan] always says: 'Bring music, and you bring life.'

Daniel Barenboim: Of course. You know, earlier this year, in May, I had organised an orchestra only of European musicians – no Israelis, no Arabs – to play a concert in Gaza. Simply to give people a little bit of relief from the harshness of their lives. And in the end the Israeli government did not allow it to happen, because they would have had to open the border to me and 35 musicians, once in the morning to let us in, once in the afternoon to let us out. We would have been there simply to make music; there was no question of anything else. But they forbade it. I found it absolutely devastating, I have to say.

Clemency Burton-Hill: What would you have played?

Daniel Barenboim: We would have played Mozart.

Clemency Burton-Hill: And if an Israeli politician had the vision to think about this differently, to say: we are a democracy, we support human rights, the inalienable human right to self-expression, we must let international musicians come here and make music freely …

Daniel Barenboim: A politician like that would not be elected in Israel.

Clemency Burton-Hill: But these are the moments, as you say, when Israel can define itself as a democracy. How can it get away with silencing something as innocuous and humane as a simple concert of Mozart in Gaza?

Daniel Barenboim: I have no idea. I have no idea. It defies every logic. Every logic. From our Jewish history we should be the first ones to know the importance of compassion and not to do unto others what was done unto us for so many centuries.

Clemency Burton-Hill: Where does it all end?

Daniel Barenboim: I don't know. I don't know. I really cannot answer that.

© Clemency Burton-Hill
39(3): 10/19
DOI: 10.1177/0306422010381042
www.indexoncensorship.org

For more information visit www.west-eastern-divan.org and www.danielbarenboim.com

SET YOURSELF FREE

Radiohead's **Colin Greenwood** explains why the band released their last album direct to their fans

It's been nearly three years since we announced our 'pay what you think it's worth' scheme for the launch of our last record *In Rainbows*. I remember the excitement of it all, not least because the release date was my wife's birthday, 10 October. The idea came from a friend of our manager, who proposed an 'honesty box', placing the onus on people to ask themselves how much they valued our music. Last summer, as we finished some more recordings, we started to think and talk about how to release them. So it seemed a good moment to take stock of the technological and cultural changes that have happened in the meantime.

In August 2007, we had finished our first record after the end of our deal with EMI. Previously, we would have given it to our record company at least three months up front, and then gone through the protracted round of meetings to decide on videos and singles – experiences we'd had for the previous six records. This time there was no EMI, and no one to decide anything but ourselves. We owned it outright, and could do whatever we wanted with it. This coincided with the growth of the internet as a medium to discover and share music, something we had used to reach fans while we made *In Rainbows*. This desire to use the technology was driven by distrust and frustration with trying to broadcast our music via traditional media, such as radio and television. Music on television is scarce, and hard to do well. Radio has such regulated playlists that disc jockeys are lucky to have one free play per show. Why go exclusively through such straitened formats when you could broadcast directly to people who are interested in you, in that moment?

The other attraction for us was the conjuring up of an event, a way of marking our releases and performances as special, unique times. The internet makes it easier for everything to be live, and that's what we do. While we were in our studio, making the last few records, we would schedule last-minute 'web casts', and, at short notice, make small, spontaneous and impromptu programmes where we would play our favourite records, talk to fans, play new and old songs live, and even cover versions of songs from bands that had inspired us. It was stitched together on old Sony cams and video editors from eBay. It did feel like a Ruritanian broadcast, but it was thrilling to be sharing a live moment with our fans that wasn't mediated by anyone except the internet service provider, and a live show that could be created ten minutes from home. I'd like to think the equivalent of this in broadcasting history would be the mom and pop radio stations that set up in America between the wars, when the excitement of a new medium was explored through the immediate community. In the same way, we saw the internet as a chance to treat the global constituency of Radiohead fans as our community. Also, it helped break up the studio tension, and made us feel less cloistered and isolated while we finished recording.

Against all this positive experience of using net technology, we'd had a bad experience on the previous record, when someone had taken some of the songs from a computer and put them online, well ahead of the official release. Everyone became very careful about carrying songs around, in the car, on CDs, music players and computers. It made you realise how easy it is to store and transmit music once it's digitised, and that the fundamental thing about music is its destiny to be broadcast or shared. Part of the process of making a record involves listening to new songs or ideas in lots of different places: the car, the kitchen, with friends late at night. Having feelings of mild anxiety about music escaping onto the web wasn't conducive to that, and there were a few panics. Fortunately, we managed to keep everything unreleased until the online download of *In Rainbows*.

The success of keeping the music off the net until release proved very powerful. A pre-digital album launch would involve some shows perhaps, record shop queues if you were lucky, and plans by the record company to mark the release as an event. In the digital world, with the ease of music escaping online, that sense of an event is diminished.

With *In Rainbows*, we were able to be the first people to digitally release our record, directly to people's personal computers, at 7.30am GMT on 10 October 2007. I was having breakfast, and watched as the file appeared in my email, and the album streamed onto my desktop. I spent the next day and night monitoring people's reactions online, both to the music and the means of delivery. Journalists in America had stayed up overnight to write the first reviews as they received the music – again, in the pre-digital age they would have had advance copies up to three weeks before. On the torrent site bulletin boards, people were arguing over whether they should be downloading and paying for the record from our site, rather than the free torrents. Various online pundits and pamphleteers were pronouncing the end of the record business, or of Radiohead, or of both.

Colin Greenwood's playlist

Reckoner
Arpeggi/Weird Fishes
Nude

Radiohead
In Rainbows
XL

For all the giddy prognostications, the most important reason for the success of *In Rainbows* was the quality of the music. I think this was overlooked, but without the great songs that we were proud of, the online release would have counted for nothing. I am optimistic that if you make good work you can secure the patronage of your fans.

Three years later, we have just finished another group of songs, and have begun to wonder about how to release them in a digital landscape that has changed again. It seems to have become harder to own music in the traditional way, on a physical object like a CD, and instead music appears the poor cousin of software, streamed or locked into a portable device like a phone or iPod. I buy hardly any CDs now and get my music from many different sources: Spotify, iTunes, blog playlists, podcasts, online streaming – reviewing this makes me realise that my appetite for music now is just as strong as when I was 13, and how dependent I am upon digital delivery. At the same time, I find a lot of the technology very frustrating and counter-intuitive. I spend a lot of time using music production software, but iTunes feels clunky. I wish it was as simple and elegant as Apple's hardware. I understand that we have become our own broadcasters and distributors, but I miss the editorialisation of music, the curatorial influences of people like John Peel or a good record label. I liked being on a record label that had us on it, along with Blur, the Beastie Boys and the Beatles.

The net is moving out of its adolescence and preparing to leave its bedroom

I'm unconvinced that the internet has replaced the club or the concert hall as a forum for people to share ideas and passions about music. Social networking models such as Twitter and foursquare are early efforts at this but have some way to go to emulate the ecosystem that labels such as Island drew upon, the interconnected club and studio worlds of managers, musicians, artists and record company mavericks, let alone pay for such a fertile environment. Shoreditch, in east London, has a vibrant scene right now, with independent labels such as Wichita, Bella Union and distribution companies like The Co-op, alongside the busy Strongroom studio. I spoke to a friend,

Dan Grech-Marguerat, about the scene. He is a busy mixer and producer, and told me that he could just sit at home and work on the computer but would miss the social buzz and benefits of working at the Strongroom and other studios.

There are signs that the net is moving out of its adolescence, and preparing to leave its bedroom. I have noticed on the fan message sites that a lot of the content and conversations have grown up, moved away from staccato chat and trolling, to discussions about artists, taste and trends, closer to writing found in music magazines.

There is less interest in the technological side of the net, and more focus on what services the web can deliver, like any other media. People are using touch and gesture-controlled devices such as the iPad to see through those objects to get to the content they want. This transparency and immediacy is exciting for us as artists, because it brings us closer to our audience.

We have yet to decide how to release our next record, but I hope these partial impressions will help give some idea of the conversations we've been having. Traditional marketplaces and media are feeling stale – supermarkets account for around 70 per cent of CDs sold in the UK, the charts are dominated by TV talent-show acts – and we are trying to find ways to put out our music that feel as good as the music itself. The ability to have a say in its release, through the new technologies, is the most empowering thing of all. ❐

©Colin Greenwood
39(3):20/24
DOI: 10.1177/0306422010379687
www.indexoncensorship.org

Colin Greenwood is Radiohead's bassist

WORDSANDMUSIC

Will Self on
God Save the Queen/Sex Pistols

In the summer of 1977 I was 15 years old and wore an old tropical linen jacket I'd bought in a charity shop for a quid. It wasn't so much off-white as ruinous, and it matched the colour of my shoes – winkle-pickers I'd painted myself using some kind of weird leather paint. Naturally I had to lie on my skinny rump to force my El Greco feet through the eight-inch ankles of my drainpipe jeans. Given all this sartorial mayhem it goes without saying that I absolutely concurred with the Sex Pistol's front man, Johnny Rotten, when he sang, 'God save the queen / The fascist regime'. Admittedly the causal connective 'it's' was lost in all the filth and the fury of his delivery, but *we* knew what he meant.

Actually, I can barely remember the circumstantial pomp that went into the celebration of the Queen's Silver Jubilee, all I can recall is the Sex Pistols' treasonable ditty, and the fact that it was banned from being played on the radio. At least I'm certain it was banned from the BBC's Radio 1. I'm not so sure about the commercial stations, but then Britain in the late 1970s still had the anomalous character of a socialist democracy with a vertiginous class system; an anomaly of which the state broadcaster was a key component.

Actually, being banned by the BBC wasn't that crushing a piece of censorship; other far more anodyne ditties used to be blanked from the charts, or have their lyrics bleeped out by reason of their mild smuttiness. And of course, like all censorship, ridding the Sex Pistols' 'God Save the Queen' from the airwaves only ensured its fizzing presence in the brainwaves of disaffected youth. Malcolm McLaren, the band's Situationist-inspired manager, got reams of publicity from the banning, together with a special cruise he organised on the day of the Jubilee, during which the band were to blast Parliament with their subversive sounds.

As I never tire of explaining to my own children, the punk era – by reason of demographics alone – was the last time when an avant-garde youth movement seriously impacted on the cultural mainstream: after that came the 1980s and the final and fully achieved crystallisation of style and profit. At least I believe that to be the case, but it may be only because I'm an old punk myself – an old punk and a middle-aged republican. If there was ever the remotest possibility of my being able to scuttle my way up the back passage of the establishment 'God Save the Queen' would act as a formidable piece of barrier contraception.

'God save the queen / 'Cos tourists are money / And our figurehead / Is not what she seems'. These lyrics may seem like furious hyperbole to some, but to me they capture perfectly the idiocy of the constitutional monarchy, an institution whose allegedly 'organic' character only serves to point up the persistently vegetative state of most of the population. Besides, what a lot there is crammed into these few short stanzas; from the Blakean invocation of 'England's dreaming', to the sneering ironic put-down 'We mean it, man', and, of course on to the bitter disruptive end in the Dadaist palilalia of 'No future, no future' over and over again.

It's difficult to imagine such tricky and subversive concepts getting an airing in contemporary pop music, but then again I'm not altogether certain I've consciously listened to contemporary pop music since the mid-1980s. And then again, the medium is always the message; the Sex Pistols were a band who excoriated their ex-record label, EMI. Now EMI is completely ex and the kids download 'God Save the Queen' as an ideologically-void curio.

'We're the flowers in the dustbin / We're the poison in your human machine'. So sang Johnny, little knowing that 30 years on he'd be aping his own conceits on a reality TV show – being banned was undoubtedly the best thing that ever happened to him, mostly it was downhill after that. ❒

©Will Self
39(3): 26/27
DOI: 10.1177/0306422010379821
www.indexoncensorship.org

Will Self's novels, short story collections and non-fiction include *The Book of Dave* (Viking), *The Butt* (Bloomsbury), *Liver: A Fictional Organ with a Surface Anatomy of Four Lobes* (Bloomsbury) and *Psycho Too* (Bloomsbury), with Ralph Steadman

THE
DEAL

If you want a career in pop music, you have to play the game. **Peter Jenner** reveals the network of censorship that underpins the industry

The popular recorded music industry is all about who controls access to the market. It's a subtle form of censorship, where the extent of a musician's freedom can depend on the degree of his or her negotiating strength and indifference to success. There is a whole army of gatekeepers collecting their share of the money and exerting influence through their knowledge of the filters (whether radio, newspapers, advertising or television) that stand between musicians and the public. After 44 years in the business as manager of musicians including Pink Floyd, Tyrannosaurus Rex, Ian Dury, Billy Bragg and Michael Franti, I have seen the difficulties that come from just doing your own thing, and the benefits from playing the game.

The usual career path for the neophyte pop star includes singing in choirs, music lessons, forming a band at school, being a DJ, making sampled compilations at home on the computer, going to college and appearing in talent shows from a very young age. Aspiring musicians then proceed to starve, live off their parents, get terrible jobs, hang out endlessly with other would-be musos as they develop their unique talent, and try to get signed by a record company, publisher or manager, or anyone else who can wave that magic wand and turn them into stars.

The problem is that the only career path for a pop musician is to become famous or rich. The only measure of success is a big bank balance, a big hit, a big car, or a big gig. Being trendy does not pay the rent, nor do great reviews. The only uniformly accepted criterion is market success. If you are a painter, novelist or serious musician, there are prizes and reviews, all of which can give you recognition, even if they don't pay the rent. There are bursaries and even the odd patron, but only in the music business are you expected to sign away the ownership of your work. In return, you get paid an advance and agree to do what is required to turn you into a hit product. It's like getting a mortgage on a house. The only problem is that even if you pay back all your advances, the company will have made plenty at the poor rates that are granted and they still own your copyright. They can decide whether to release your work or promote it for the full length of copyright (a long and occasionally lengthening period of time).

The essentials of the deal are simple. The record companies want hits, and that means getting records on the radio. To get played, the aspiring artist's record should not sound too different from the rest of the playlist to maintain the station's ratings. This leads to negative programming, where the key aim is to ensure that people do not switch channels. To keep their audience, stations will broadcast uniform music, while the industry puts a lot of effort into choosing songwriters, musicians, engineers and producers who are all 'today's sound'. Once radio, press and television have decided an artist is the next big thing, it often becomes a self-fulfilling prophecy, because that is the message the public gets.

It is like betting on horse races. You look at the breeding, the trainer, the jockey, the owner, the recent form and the other horses in the race, and then you place your bet. The biggest bet is on the US charts and the second biggest is on the UK charts, as success in these two markets is a benchmark for the rest of the world. It then becomes easier to break into other markets, as the infrastructure has already been built: the recording, artwork, photos, videos, biogs, clothes and haircuts. All that is required locally is the operating costs. The stakes may be enormous, but the pay-off is huge.

The costs of marketing have spiralled as the media have multiplied. The number of recordings has increased due to the ease of making them and the incredible reduction in price. As a result, the cost of launching a new act has grown while the market has shrunk: the multiplication of media and media consumption now makes it harder to advertise to a mass audience. The worst aspect of this is that the middle sellers have become less profitable, while there are fewer big hits. All this increases the pressure on producing hits, and to take as few risks as possible. Any artist who wants to make a living has to play within these rules.

In the UK and US there is also an assumption that people will only listen to songs in English, so any non-English speaker is expected to write and sing in English if they want to break into these critical markets. This also applies to singers who speak minority languages in other countries: they will have to sing in English rather than in their own language. The same principle applies to the language of music itself. Hence the dominance of the three-minute single in most western countries: built around verse/chorus/middle-eight repetitive structures, it makes it hard for any other musical form to get heard.

The pressure to write within conventional boundaries also stretches into the content of lyrics. Writing about war, death, illness, social inequalities and taboo subjects is not likely to get you anywhere. Happy, positive music is preferred, and the ideal content is the discussion of individual relationships of a heterosexual nature, but without too much controversial detail. There are, of course, occasional exceptions that prove this rule, but anyone addressing serious and controversial issues is unlikely to get a contract or exposure for their work.

This gets to the heart of the contradictions within the music business. The public is always looking for something new, and just like any other fashion commodity the change must not be too great. So we see solo girl singers being the thing, boy indie guitar bands, teen boy bands, dance music or the latest 'pop idol'.

Occasionally the zeitgeist shifts and outsiders break into the mainstream. Punk was a classic case of this. Throughout the early punk era it was virtually impossible to get acts signed to major labels or their records played, until the public voted with their wallets. Most of the punk records were put

Peter Jenner's playlist

Sex and Drugs and Rock and Roll
Ian Dury
Stiff Records

Between the Wars
Billy Bragg
Go! Discs

Television, the Drug of the Nation
Disposable Heroes of Hiphoprisy
Island Records

An exception that proves the rule: Ian Dury and the Blockheads, Cardiff, 1978
Credit: Trinity Mirror/Mirrorpix/Alamy

out by small indie labels, and it was some time before they were available in all record stores. My partner and I financed Ian Dury's recordings and it was impossible to get a deal, so we ended up with our friends on the new and 'groovy' Stiff Records, and licensed the record to them. 'Sex and Drugs and Rock and Roll' never got played on the radio, while 'Hit Me with Your Rhythm Stick' was a smash.

Ironically, the BBC went on to ban Stiff's other huge record, Frankie Goes to Hollywood's 'Relax', which got publicly and explicitly banned, much to the label's delight. The establishment learnt from this that it was better not to ban undesirable records, simply to ignore them.

So when Ian Dury's 'Spasticus Autisticus' was released in the Year of the Disabled in 1981, radio stations would not play it as it might 'cause offence', despite the fact that it was the first new record by a big star of the time. There were no objections from any disability groups, it was only objected to by radio programmers.

Similarly, the political zeitgeist can sometimes make way for a musician whose lack of commercial appeal is part of the attraction. Billy Bragg's instinctive relationship with the unions during the miners' struggles with Margaret Thatcher in the 80s turned him into a hit artist and a symbol of resistance, despite never getting much airplay or mass exposure. The album *Life's a Riot* became a hit on the back of John Peel and other underground DJs' support, along with the music press's coverage and word of mouth. GLC gigs and Kirsty MacColl's version of 'New England' also helped to make his name. But Billy has never had a huge single or album, despite selling steadily in many countries over the years.

The digital revolution at first appeared to challenge the traditional controls, but online patterns of usage now appear to mimic offline behaviour. Although some of the more minority musical groupings, such as surf punk, grime, techno and death metal, do communicate internationally online, and have started to build their own economies and career paths, so far they have stayed marginal. When they become popular, they are liable to be absorbed by the creative industries and be sanitised for the mass market, as happened with The Clash, Pink Floyd and the Sex Pistols. This has of course also been the case with minority labels in the past, including Mute, Rough Trade, Virgin, Chrysalis and Island, where they have been absorbed into the mainstream.

The leading cultural institutions are managing to maintain control over the internet, so the traditional power base continues to survive: whether it is the big sites like the BBC or the *Guardian*; the methods of payment which ensure that only those in the system can hope to get paid from internet use, or the marginalisation of new artists within sites that the major labels will not license.

Even illegal music services are failing to buck the conservative trend. The big hits are usually no different from the hits in the traditional media. The established marketing systems seem to be remarkably adept at maintaining their control. The campaign against 'piracy' and the dominance of licensing services in a cumbersome and expensive manner have had the effect of limiting the reach of the new media in economic terms. The way that sites are bought up by traditional media, whether MySpace, Friends Reunited or Last FM, or need huge inputs of venture capital money, as in the case of Google and Amazon, all suggests that while the media platforms may change, ownership will remain in the same hands.

This was always the case, from the days of the Rolling Stones, Jimi Hendrix and Pink Floyd, through to the punks, reggae, hip hop and dance music; one of the keys to the success of the modern capitalist system is the way it can absorb subversive movements and seduce them with cash and power.

Just as the communist and fascist regimes of the past understood the importance of popular culture, maintaining an acceptable version of it for the masses to prevent dangerous ideas undermining the status quo in the guise of culture, so the capitalist system has found its own methods of cultural control. The essential method is to control access to the market, so that financial intermediaries can filter what comes through. It is interesting that the whole debate about 'piracy' on the internet is really about control of content. If creation and distribution of content are too easy then the system is threatened. That in turn threatens the very heart of capitalism.

Intellectual property is a concept that is designed to provide monopoly profits to the owners of that property, and that structure of rights is what attracts the investment at the heart of the whole system. A world without brands, trademarks, patents or copyrights would not be capitalism as we know it. The whole principle of competition and markets is to get rid of competitors and exercise control. To some extent that is what has happened in the music industry in the last 50 years and that is why there is such resistance to filesharing.

Censorship in the digital world will become more subtle, just as it did in the world of mass communication. The illusion of free expression needs to be maintained, but it will always be a struggle to challenge the basic economic and power structures that run our 'free society'. Censorship is both positive and negative. It projects and promotes acceptable attitudes and views, and within those parameters it permits considerable freedom. But ideas that really challenge those existing power structures will find it hard to be heard, and that is a more effective way of dealing with dissident opinion than banning those views.

The good news though is that it is possible to marginally nudge radical issues and ideas along, but it is painful and it is hard. The important point is not to believe the hype that we are a free society, and that culture is open and available for all. 'Know your enemy' is always good advice. ❑

©Peter Jenner
39(3): 28/33
DOI: 10.1177/0306422010382705
www.indexoncensorship.org

Peter Jenner is legendary in the music business as manager to Pink Floyd, The Clash and Billy Bragg, amongst others. He is a digital rights expert, president emeritus of the International Music Managers' Forum, director of UK MMF and on the advisory board of Featured Artists Coalition

BANNED: A ROUGH GUIDE

Marie Korpe and **Ole Reitov** have been tracking the music censors and the censored for more than a decade. They reflect on the tactics of modern censorship

When we founded Freemuse ten years ago, our aim was to defend freedom of expression for musicians and composers. Since then, we have documented music censorship in more than 100 countries. At first, we were not aware of the size of the problem, but the longer we have worked in the field, the larger the challenges become. Maybe we are still only seeing the tip of the iceberg. While more journalists have got music censorship on their radar and a number of musicians have benefited from our support, it is still rare to find records of music censorship and violations of musicians' rights to freedom of expression in reports from Amnesty, Human Rights Watch and other global free expression watchdogs. It is still rare to find mention of these violations in reports from embassies, and so far no organisation accredited to the United Nations has raised these issues during the sessions of the United Nations Universal Periodic Review. The silence from the music industry and organisations representing musicians and composers still astonishes us, as if the problem didn't exist. What follows below are scenes from our journey over the past 30 years through the landscape of music and censorship.

Desert of solitude: self-censorship in Pakistan, 1979–1980

'I cannot perform in public as long as my youngest daughter is not married,' said singer and actress Iqbal Bano. 'A "decent family" would never marry their son to the daughter of a woman who is performing in public, so this is why I can only sing for you here in a private setting.' The harmonium player set the tone and Iqbal Bano began singing:

> *dasht-e-tanhaai mein, ai jaan-e-jahaan, larzaan hain*
> In the desert of my solitude, oh love of my life, quiver

These are the words of Pakistan's beloved Urdu poet Faiz Ahmad Faiz, the intellectual socialist who never ceased to criticise corrupt leaders and generals and is known to millions as a master of *ghazals* – the semi-classical poetic songs which transcend boundaries of gender and age and have reached illiterate Pakistanis as well as the educated upper classes.

We were sitting in the house of one of Pakistan's most famous lawyers, Raza Kazim, a good friend of Faiz, with whom he shared revolutionary ideas and a passion for music. This was the first time that we had encountered the censorship of music and it opened our eyes. Kazim, renowned for his intellectual sharpness, had built his own music studio, sponsored musicians, developed new musical instruments and was a scholar on the role of Muslim musicians in the development of North Indian classical music. Kazim had invited us to his studio to exchange views and experiences on recording techniques and the arts in general.

Iqbal Bano was able to perform in this 'safe music house' in Lahore. Loved by millions across Pakistan as one of the most distinguished *ghazal* singers of the sub-continent, she had voluntarily abstained from public performances until her daughter found a suitable husband.

From 1979, the political and religious environment in Pakistan was extremely hostile towards music, dance and most other art forms. After seizing power in 1977, General Zia ul Haq had started using religion as a tool for his own abuse of power and easily found willing religious leaders as allies against all kinds of 'spiritual pollution'. He introduced Islamic law, thousands of boys joined the *mohalla* (local religious) schools and in an attempt to 'correct' wrong interpretations of Islam, the government banned a parade in the autumn of 1979 of Sufi musicians and dancers travelling from Rawalpindi to the small village Shahan Nurpur, one of the Sufi centres of the country. But the general and the army did not dare attack the hundreds of Sufi followers as they danced and sang through the broad avenues of the capital – a small victory for unauthorised Islam.

Was Iqbal Bano, the former film star and winner of several awards, a victim of Zia ul Haq's terror regime? Most probably not. She simply shared the destiny of hundreds of talented women performers. Her 'self-imposed' censorship was a result of the complex cultural, religious and social conflicts of many societies, where music is considered a great joy, but musicians and performers are considered 'low caste'. This was little different from Europe, where daughters of rich families learned to play and sing but were not necessarily expected to make a career of it. So Iqbal, with that remarkable voice, was still climbing the ladder from being considered a 'courtesan' to becoming a respectable woman.

> In the desert of my solitude,
> Beneath the dust and ashes of distance
> Bloom the jasmines and roses of your proximity

Iqbal Bano's voice was joined by the tabla player. She recited with a sense of bitter sweetness; her voice had thrilled audiences all over the sub-continent. We double-checked the tape recorder – this was her most famous song – we didn't want to miss a single breath, a single phrase.

> The sun of separation has set
> And the night of union has arrived.

When her daughter got married, Iqbal Bano returned to her public. Breaking the ban on performing the revolutionary songs by Faiz Ahmed Faiz, she gained cult status in 1985 when she performed the inspirational anthem 'Hum Dekhenge' (We Will See), a song that became a symbol of resistance, in a recorded concert in front of an audience. Iqbal Bano died in 2009.

Music is bad for your health: Africa and Asia, early 1980s

After living in Pakistan for a year, we set off for a three-year broadcasting and research programme on local music industries around the world, and travelled to Sri Lanka, Kenya, Tunisia and Tanzania. One pattern was striking – in each country there was tight media control and oppositional voices were not very willing to talk while the tape recorder was switched on. Censorship was widespread and artists were rather unwilling to discuss it. What we had experienced in Pakistan was not

Revellers dancing to music at a wedding, October 2001. Under the Taliban, the activity was banned
Credit: Martin Adler/Panos

unique. Religious forces and political leaders kept a firm grip not only on the media, but even on the arts scene. Censorship had suddenly become an embedded theme in our work – we were both journalists covering music and current affairs. But in those pre-web days we were unable to find a lot of material on the subject, apart from reports on increasing censorship in apartheid South Africa.

In Tanzania, we visited the small bookshop of a shabby four-star hotel. Our eyes were attracted by the title of a booklet, *Music and Its Effects*, published in 1974 (http://www.islamic-laws.org/musicanditseffect.htm). The first chapter, 'What is music?', told us that music, according to the 'new national diction-ary', was the 'art of combining sounds or sequences of notes into harmonious patterns pleasing to the ear and satisfying to the emotions'. Then we read the third paragraph: 'In Islam, music is called *ghina* and in sharia law it is counted as one of the "great sins"'. 'A brisk and lively musical programme, in particular if it is accompanied by musical instruments, disturbs the equilibrium of the various systems; digestion is badly affected; palpitation of the heart is increased; blood pressure increases and abnormal secretion of harmones [sic] leaves a lasting effect upon general health.'

A few blocks away from the bookshop, Radio Freedom, the exile radio of the ANC, was producing revolutionary programmes, and we heard samples of music banned from South Africa – a great contrast to state-controlled radio.

The birth of Freemuse, 1997-2000

When the Rushdie affair exploded in 1989, media all over the world started focusing on threats against writers. While famous authors have defended Rushdie and Taslima Nasrin, who has faced similar problems in Bangladesh, famous musicians run campaigns against hunger and other good causes – but neither Bono, Sting or Bob Geldof are out there defending their musical colleagues. The music industry and music media seem to have a blind spot.

In the autumn of 1997, we decided to organise the world's first-ever conference on music censorship from our base in Copenhagen. The Danish Institute for Human Rights supported the idea and became a partner, Danish Broadcasting offered office space and the Danish minister of culture, Elsebeth Gerner Nielsen, provided funding to gather banned musicians, human rights lawyers, the media and scholars for a world conference on music and censorship. Ursula Owen, then chief executive of Index on Censorship, liked the idea of collaborating on a special *Index* issue on music and censorship, 'Smashed Hits' (*Index* 6/98), for the conference.

The opening session set the tone. Cecile Pracher, a former censor from SABC, the South African Broadcasting Corporation, sat next to Ray Phiri (of Graceland fame) and Sipho Mabuse. She explained why and how their music was banned. 'It was very simple,' she said. 'We had 13 rules and if the lyrics, the musical style or the combination of musicians were violating these rules, we just banned it and scratched the tracks on the vinyl.'

The participants agreed that it was not sufficient to protest against censorship. We needed to analyse, document and understand the effects and create space for dialogue. A small group of dedicated conference participants decided to set up an organisation to defend freedom of expression for musicians and composers. Freemuse – the first and so far only international organisation advocating freedom of musical expression – was born. After two years of hard work fundraising, the Freemuse office was set up in Copenhagen in August 2000, with the aim of documenting violations of freedom of expression against musicians and to advocate their rights.

The first Freemuse report, 'Can you stop the birds singing?', was published the following year. Written by Professor John Baily, it was quoted in more than 50 countries and became an eye-opener for many. A country without music? Is this possible?

For a period, the Taliban exercised severe music control in Afghanistan and the old idea of music as a 'tool of the devil' was getting increasing support from radical religious groups, spreading to Sudan, Pakistan, Somalia and pockets of Europe and Africa. The idea of the negative effect of music is not new. Plato wrote that 'music is seductive' and therefore music that stimulated negative behaviour should be controlled. Christian missionaries banned drums in Africa and Greenland. Swedish fiddle players were told to burn their instruments in the late 19th century and Stalin, Hitler and McCarthy had various pretexts for banning artists and musical expression they didn't like. Somehow history repeats itself, but underneath the mechanisms is the same aim: control.

Musicians under fire: Nigeria, 2000

In the northern Kano state, sharia law had been implemented. This had a harsh impact on local musicians, who reported that they were being molested and their equipment and loudspeakers broken by the local *hisbas* (religious militias). Ali Bature, a tall, proud state bureaucrat, did not question sharia but in his view there were 'regulations and regulations'. He believed that if something was banned people should know why and if something was allowed it should also be safe for artists to perform. In 2002, a censorship board was set up in Kano, ironically in the name of protecting the Hausa musicians.

Freemuse sent French journalist J C Servant to Nigeria to investigate the mechanisms and impact of censorship. Bature, a member of the censorship board, explained: 'The role of this office is to maintain and to protect the culture of the people in Kano.' Having travelled the country, Servant wrote in his report: 'Kano's cultural interaction appears to be the exception that proves the rule in the north. Elsewhere an insidious campaign against musicians and music censorship appears to be gaining ground.'

Femi Kuti, whose song 'Beng Beng Beng' was banned by the authorities (see pages 108-111) and who is the son of the legendary Fela Kuti, told Freemuse: 'A band like my band cannot play in the north. The dancers would be stoned to death and I would be persecuted.' But in the south, Pentecostals were also gaining ground as public guardians of morality. Femi Kuti continued: 'It's more difficult to talk about sex or religion than politics today in Nigeria. Although they work hand in hand, it has been so embedded in the system that nobody can do anything with religion, and if you are against any of the religious bodies, Islam or Christianity, automatically you are an outcast in society.'

All that is banned is desired: Beirut, 2005

They were all there: Marcel Khalife, the Lebanese oud maestro, who went on trial for quoting a verse of the Quran in one of his songs; Salman Ahmad, the Pakistani rock star, whose band Junoon was censored for protesting against nuclear tests and political corruption; Syria's famous filmmaker Mohamad Malas, whose film about music, *The Passion*, had been banned; Davey D, the walking hip-hop encyclopaedia; and Iran's amazing vocalist Mahsa Vahdat, who cannot perform in her home country. Freemuse and the Middle East Office of the Heinrich Böll Foundation were hosting a conference on music censorship. Mai Ghoussoub, artist and founder of Saqi Books, quoted a phrase she loved as a child in her keynote speech: 'It is banned to ban.'

Remembering the small booklet *Music and Its Effects*, published by the Bilal Mission in Tanzania, one of the spearheads for missionaries of radical Islam, we were all looking forward to hearing the perspective of the respected Islamic scholar Sheikh Ibrahim Ramadan al Mardini of the Beirut Studies and Documentation Centre. We had asked Sheikh al Mardini to discuss music and Islam with a representative from Hamas, who suddenly had to go to Mecca.

'There is no ban on music in the Quran and those talking about which music is *haram* and which music is *halal* have very weak evidence', said al Mardini. 'Censorship has turned into a totalitarian tool, which is preserving the existence of regimes.' Mardini totally rejected censorship and said that religious leaders can guide people, but not ban anything. The report summing up the conference in Beirut easily found its title from an Arabic proverb: 'All that is banned is desired'.

Dirty tricks: Gothenburg, Sweden, 2006

In South Africa, Calvinism inspired the architects of apartheid, so obviously lyrics propagating nihilism were banned. But it is one thing to physically scratch a 33rpm vinyl with a needle, another to stop the career of musicians with more violent methods.

The Freemuse-sponsored film *Stopping the Music*, produced by Michael Drewett at Grahamstown University in South Africa and premiered during the second world conference on music and censorship in 2002, revealed

Femi Kuti performs as part of celebrations for Africa Day, Johannesburg, South Africa, 25 May 2007
Credit: Siphiwe Sibeko/Reuters

how the secret police in South Africa destroyed the career of Roger Lucey, one of the country's most promising singer-songwriters,. In the film, Lucey came face to face with Paul Erasmus for the first time, the police agent behind the 'dirty tricks business'. Lucey and Erasmus attended the premier and opened the conference.

Drewett had curated an exhibition on music censorship, and when this was shown at the Museum of World Cultures in Gothenburg, we invited the two former combatants to talk about the film and their lives in front of an audience. This was their fifth public encounter in five years since Freemuse had first introduced them to each other. The former enemies had become reconciled. Documenting and understanding the mechanisms and effects of censorship is one of the prime activities of Freemuse. This was a chance to complement our material.

We were doing another interview with Erasmus in the cafeteria of the museum. In a few moments he would be sitting with Lucey in front of an audience and trying to tell why and how he, a white policeman, got involved in the destruction of the white protest singer Roger Lucey.

Lucey came by. 'You need a beer, Paul?' he asked. Paul nodded and continued the interview. 'I even threatened to open a file on one of the members of my family because he talked about "right and wrong". In those days you were either for or against the apartheid regime.'

He recalled another incident, when he walked into the office of the record company that released Lucey's music and said to the company executive: 'This Roger Lucey is a communist and is going to be detained, so you are not going to produce his music anymore!' That worked. Paul was in the 'dirty tricks' department of South Africa's much feared and brutal special branch dealing with dissidents. He had a licence to use any method necessary to 'destroy the filth'. 'Yeah, that was the term we used. Roger had been interviewed by Voice of America and one of our seniors simply told me to stop "this filth".' Tapping Roger Lucey's telephone, Erasmus and his colleagues always knew where Lucey was going. But why spend a lot of time and energy on a long-haired dissident 'communist voice' who criticised the apartheid regime, when things could be settled quickly and easy?

Getting bored of the usual 'in the middle of the night house search' to scare the guy, Erasmus decided to make a spectacular move. Why not throw a bit of tear gas into a club while 'that Lucey' was performing one of his 'communist songs'? Erasmus and a couple of buddies did their usual pub visit, had a few beers and threw a bit of tear gas into Jo'burg's well-known Mangles club, where the upcoming 'Dylan of South Africa' was performing for a crowded house. And that did it, says Erasmus: 'After the tear gas thing at the Mangles Club – when we talked to the club owners – the last thing they needed was a show stopped by beefy police guys. Remember, the terrorist war had started. So we told these people: "Look, if you are going to have that bastard communist play we'll blow

Marie Korpe and Ole Reitov's playlist

Dasht-e-Tanhae Mein
Iqbal Bano
Available on YouTube

Alisero
Ferhat Tunç
Grappa

Beng Beng Beng
Femi Kuti
Universal Music

your bloody place." So after Mangles, I think they stopped his show within a week.'

Erasmus, who later came forward during the South African reconciliation process, could have killed Lucey. He almost did. Lucey was deprived of his promising career and became a self-destructive addict. Lucey did not even know that he was the target of the secret police. His friends told him not to 'overestimate his importance', so Lucey was completely unaware of the dirty tricks business until Erasmus called him many years later and told him: 'Look Roger, all these things happened and I am to blame for this. What can I say? I am really sorry.'

Recalling those days when he was more than happy to serve as a communist hunter he said: 'I grew up with communism being Satanic. It was the hammer and sickle or the cross. I gave money to people claiming to bring Bibles into communist countries. I always saw this horde of people taking over Africa. We almost had nightmares like during the First World War, shooting hordes of communists who just keep coming. Those were the images. You know growing up in this Calvinistic, apartheid system we thought they wanted our oranges, our churches and they were anti-Christ. Reading the books of Karl Marx would be the end of the world.'

Erasmus is now a farmer trying to get on with his life and has totally distanced himself from his work. 'I haven't reconciled with myself, I don't know how to,' he said. 'I really devastated my life. I knew exactly what I was doing and I was tricked by the power, there is no excuse for that. You know, Roger, in my mind, was not a person – he represented communism. Anything anti-national was labelled communist and the rock musicians represented the collapse of morals. Lennon was a communist, underground was Satanic, yeah, music was the most dangerous thing. Why music? we asked. 'It is an expression of the soul. And it reaches people who can't read.'

Music on trial: Izmir, Turkey, 2007

The Freemuse website, www.freemuse.org, launched in 2001. The first musician to link to it was the Turkish singer Ferhat Tunç, who has constantly struggled for freedom of expression and faced numerous court cases. We invited him to the world music expo Womex, in Germany in 2004, a country where he had earlier spent several years in exile during the Turkish military regime. At the third Freemuse World Conference in Istanbul in 2006, and a couple of court cases later, he was one of the speakers. We discussed how Freemuse could create more awareness about the situation in Turkey in general and for musicians in particular. One year later there was a dramatic court case against Tunç (see pp.131-139).

Mahsa Vahdat at the Index on Censorship Freedom of Expression Awards, London, March 2010
Credit: Karim Merie

When Tunç entered the Izmir tenth high criminal court, the court-room was completely packed and the front row was occupied by ten police officers armed with machine guns. Ferhat Tunç stood facing the judges, who were on a podium six feet above him with the prosecutor. Although this was neither the first nor the last time the popular Kurdish singer and writer appeared in court, the charges this time were really serious. Tunç was accused of 'making propaganda for a terrorist organisation'. The new case against him was triggered by his remarks during a concert in Alanya on 22 July 2006, where Tunç mentioned the Kurdish issue and demanded a peaceful solution. The indictment quoted Ferhat Tunç as saying: 'Each killed guerrilla is a son of this country too. I feel sorry for each killed soldier and also for each guerrilla.' The prosecutor demanded 15 years imprisonment and the atmosphere in the courtroom was tense as the main judge threw out one of the onlookers who forgot to switch off his cell phone.

Observing the trial, Freemuse was joined by a small delegation which included Jens Peter Bonde, president of the EU Democrats, and senior political advisor Selma Kiliçer from the EU Commission office in Ankara. The prosecutor read the charges. Tunç was requested to present his version. He started by talking about Turkish history. After six minutes, the main judge interrupted him and said: 'Mr. Tunç, you are not here to give the court a history lesson.'

Tunç replied: 'With due respect, sir, but in order to give perspective to these charges I need to go back in history.' Then he continued for another 20 minutes. His lawyer, who had 12 assistant lawyers, then demanded Tunç's immediate release and requested the prosecutor to present witnesses.

But there were no witnesses. The two policemen who reported the 'incident' had not been called to the court. After some discussion, the three judges left the court room and return after five minutes. Then the prosecutor said that due to lack of evidence he wished to withdraw the case for the moment. Everyone in the courtroom held their breath. Was this the much feared, so-called 'deep state' of Turkey at its worst? Once again the judges left the room. Five minutes later they returned and the main judge announced that Ferhat was acquitted.

Outside the court there was a massive media reception. European parliamentarian Jans Peter Bonde spoke: 'Freedom of speech is one of the fundamental freedoms in the Council of Europe's Convention for the Protection of Human Rights, which Turkey has joined and is therefore obliged to follow. It is also a condition for EU membership. This membership moves closer with Ferhat Tunç's acquittal.'

After all the media interviews, Ferhat took his friends to a restaurant in a beautiful mountain setting. We talked to the Scandinavian media and Ferhat called his wife in Istanbul. 'I was acquitted,' he said.

'I know,' she replied. 'I saw it all on TV.' Three years later, the 'deep state' is running new cases against Ferhat. It never stops. And with Web 2.0, the whole world can now watch and read. ❒

© Marie Korpe and Ole Reitov
39(3): 34/45
DOI: 10.1177/0306422010381043
www.indexoncensorship.org

For further information go to www.freemuse.org

FIGHT THE POWER

Hip hop has replaced folk as the number-one sound for protest music. **Malu Halasa** reports on its global appeal from the US to Iran

Some 30 years after its inception with the 1979 release of 'Rapper's Delight' by the Sugarhill Gang, hip hop has emerged as the sound of worldwide dissent. Before performing 'Language of Violence' by Disposable Heroes of Hiphoprisy for an evening of protest songs at the Southbank's Meltdown festival last June, in London, gay rocker Tom Robinson said people were wondering where the Bob Dylans of today were and suggested that protest singers are no longer in folk but hip hop. Rappers in Burma, Algeria, China, Senegal and Iran, to name a few of the countries, all use a relatively simple but effective formula of beats and rhymes to analyse, criticise and threaten their respective status quos.

The transition of hip hop from a cut and paste music forged in the American ghetto to a sound of global expression is a story very much rooted in the music's low tech, minimal approach. DJs isolated break beats or instrumental breaks sometimes using two turntables, other times tape machines, while MCs or rappers, some as young as 14 or 16, formulated the perfect rhyme that fit over an amalgamation of cut-up sound. Sometimes the backing would be a simple musical loop, scratching or just noises

Public Enemy, Montreux, Switzerland, May 1988
Credit: Andre Csillag/Rex Features

somebody made with their mouth. It was a new, cheaper way of making what could potentially sound like sophisticated music that wasn't as rigid as a three-minute pop song. During live performance, impromptu breaks and freestyle verses were constantly added. At my first rap gig, at the Audubon Ballroom in 1980, where Malcolm X had been assassinated 15 years earlier, there were so many DJs and rappers on stage that no one could figure out if Grandmaster Flash was a person or a posse.

Serviced by a small but active independent record scene, hip hop would have probably stayed a cult endeavour within the orbit of New York/New Jersey if not for the commercial success of the Def Jam label in the 1980s, which capitalised on the music's essentials. It was Def Jam's act, Run-DMC, and their song 'My Addis' that was the first instance of hip hop going global, which melded rap's distinctive sound to a fashion brand. After that, no matter your ethnicity or language, everyone pretty much knew the allure of gold chains and trainers.

But more important than the music's obvious commercial intentions was its attitude. Another Def Jam act, Public Enemy, embodied rebellion in the form of slamming beats and highly politicised lyrics. Their songs 'Rebel without a Pause' and 'Fight the Power', about race, religion and the politics of a disenfranchised people, remain inspirational hip-hop anthems to all who hear them today.

In different countries around the world, the rappers who fight the power are, metaphorically speaking, the children of Public Enemy. In his song 'Prince of Persia', Reveal, aka Mehrak Golestan, from the group Poisonous Poets, uses English slang and Farsi to criticise western attitudes towards Iran and the wider Middle East. Early in the song he says that he 'built [his] studio in Takhte Jamshid' (ancient ruins in Persepolis), then later continues: 'U couldn't get close cos you lack the agility/Fuck the army my crew roll paramilitary/U don't wanna come to Iran to see me/You might get kidnapped and beheaded on TV/I roam the streets of the Middle East freely/All I need is weed and a little tick beanie.'

Reveal, 26, was born in Iran. Despite growing up in London he has strong ties to the rap scene in Tehran. With Iranian rapper Hich-Kas, who does a cameo performance in Bahman Ghobadi's film *No One Knows about Persian Cats*, he recorded 'Trippe Maa' (Our Style), the first Iranian rap song to feature live Persian classical instrumentation, which was recorded, mixed and released to a professional standard, with a video – the first time ever for Iranian hip hop. In May, Reveal and Hich-Kas performed together in Kuala Lumpur and are now working on putting together a tour. Reveal also works with composer Mahdyar who mixes Persian licks with hardcore beats.

He believes that hip hop's emergence as the global voice of dissent is due to the fact that 'expressing yourself in hip hop is a lot more straightforward and easy than perhaps in other art forms – not just music but painting, dance, whatever – because in those forms experience is abstracted. Hip hop is direct'.

Malu Halasa's playlist

Trippe maa
Hich-Kas and Reveal
Available on YouTube

Obama Nation
Lowkey
Mesopotamia Music

Language of Violence
Disposable Heroes of Hiphoprisy
Island Records

This is emphasised, he feels, by the point of view in the genre. Rock or pop songs allow for other points of view, not necessarily those of the singer, while hip hop songs, he stresses, are always 'in the first person and very much rooted in the here and now'.

Marry this with the space available in hip-hop songs and the result is a musical form tailor-made for complex content. Reveal explains, 'I personally think that no other musical form has the content of hip hop. Hip-hop lyrics are not repetitive, they're like verses, they progress. You might have a song with two 48-bar verses with two eight-bar choruses compared to your average rock or pop song of mostly eight bars of lyrics. There is a lot more content in hip hop.'

Its relatively uncomplicated construction makes it appealing to rappers, DJs and musicians who may not necessarily speak English and come from radically different musical cultures. 'It's a form of music that doesn't take much to do.' Reveal concludes, 'You don't need to know how to play an instrument or to buy new equipment. Literally, it's poetry – words and ideas. It's a very natural extension of writing and appeals to young people because it's exciting – it has the rhythm and the rhyme form. It does what it says on the tin.' ❏

©Malu Halasa
39(3): 46/49
DOI: 10.1177/0306422010379803
www.indexoncensorship.org

Malu Halasa is an author, editor and journalist. Her books include *Transit Tehran* (Garnet) and *The Secret Life of Syrian Lingerie* (Chronicle). She was one of the foremost journalists writing about rap for the British music press in the 1980s

TRUST
MONEY, MARKETS AND SOCIETY
GEOFFREY HOSKING

WHO DO YOU THINK YOU ARE?
THE SEARCH FOR ARGENTINA'S LOST CHILDREN
ANDREW GRAHAM-YOOL

HUMANITARIAN ASSISTANCE?
HAITI AND BEYOND
NEIL MIDDLETON

HISTORY THIEVES
ZINOVY ZINIK

THAT'S OFFENSIVE!
CRITICISM, IDENTITY, RESPECT
STEFAN COLLINI

Seagull
BOOKS

SOUNDS OF SILENCE

In a culture where pop music can only thrive underground, Iranians have to defy convention to create their own music. **Negar Shaghaghi** reports

I quickly took the tape from my friend, who was sitting next to me in the classroom, and carefully put it in my backpack among my textbooks. My heart was pounding so hard I could hear it. With my sweaty hands I picked up my pen and tried to remember the last thing the science teacher had said about the formation of cells in a plant. My mind, though, was filled with thoughts of the tape in my bag, waiting for me to take it home, analyse it, read its label that said 'Nirvana', then put it in the tape player and listen to it, while checking the name of the first track from the list written on the back of the tape in black ink.

This is one of the few vivid memories I have from my early teenage years in Tehran in the mid-1990s. Coming from a strict, academic family, whose musical tastes never went beyond classical music, my only source of anything modern was friends who had a satellite television which allowed them to watch MTV and other music channels; or relatives who travelled outside Iran and came back with a cassette or two of what they believed was good music.

Music videos of MTV chart hits were recorded on VHS and copied several times and spread among friends. Original leaflets and posters were copied in a print shop near school to go on walls or above our beds. The excitement of going home to watch or listen to music was heightened by the fear of getting caught by the principal of our girls' school, which had a strict religious and moral code. In a society where you were stopped and searched and even prosecuted for having so-called 'illegal' tapes and for playing music in your car, being caught by the principal would not be without consequences – being expelled or at least spending hours in her office listening to her criticising your parents for raising a rebellious daughter with no respect for morality.

Despite the harsh consequences, the search for music went beyond the walls of the elementary schools into the black market of the high street in northern and central Tehran. The kinds of music that could be found there were either Iranian or western, including pirated recordings of pop singers who had fled to California after the Islamic revolution of 1979 and were still producing music. Although it was of poor quality in terms of musicality and production, it fed the nostalgia of the older generation and reminded them of the cabaret and club nights of the 70s. Western music, on the other hand, could be anything from techno and pop to Nirvana and Black Sabbath. The popularity of western music could be seen in the graffiti that covered many walls in Tehran. Alongside the 'Down with ...' graffiti slogans were the names of bands such as Metallica, sometimes misspelled as 'Metalika'. Often you would see someone's first name put together with the name of his favourite band – Ali Metallica or Saman Zeppelin – a nickname given to them by friends.

Music was spread among people by word of mouth and hand to hand. Limited sources meant that people listened to similar artists, bands such as Pink Floyd, Portishead, Eloy and Led Zeppelin. This kind of alternative music seemed to express the innermost feelings of young people in a country that, in little more than a decade, had faced revolution, war, a collapsing economy and a dramatic cultural shift. This was a society where even imported dried milk could only be purchased on the black market at a high price, and where huge adjustments were still being made to the new cultural regulations imposed after the revolution. All these elements led Iran to become an isolated society within the international community.

Alternative music, which itself represented a form of isolation and deconstruction, became young people's response to this social exclusion. The period when alternative music became influential on the global music scene was also the post-war period in Iran (the Iran-Iraq war ended in 1988) when young people were trying to put a war behind them that had lasted eight years and seen one million casualties on the Iranian side alone, and were seeking to feed their souls with the sound of music. Heavy metal and later alternative music, such as Slayer and Tool, became the new language of a generation that was bursting with emotion, but had to come home to parents always struggling to overcome financial hardships and an altered culture.

Musical tastes in the 90s closely resembled those of young people in eastern European countries, such as heavy metal fans in Poland. Their preference was for music that encouraged introspection; I would say it reflected their solitude. Alternative music in essence was known for its rejection of the commercialisation of mainstream culture. The definition of commercialisation may differ from one society to another, but alternative music responds to sentiments common to people all over the world. The reaction of these young, emotional Iranians was not aggressive, but sprang from deep within. As in Iran's ancient culture, the response to sadness and sorrow is usually a poem that expresses your innermost feelings. For example, the Mughal massacre in Iran in 1221 is widely reflected in Mowlana's poetry of the period.

Music became a tool with which to fight western imperialism

Yet music had to be listened to in private. In a country with a history of poetry more than a thousand years old, as well as a jazz and prog-rock scene in the late 60s and early 70s, the only thing that could be heard was a disturbing but constant silence. It was not that people did not try to break this silence, but in a country where wearing jeans was condemned as importing western culture, the consequences of playing or performing music were even harsher. In other words, music that in essence is an emotional tool for representing feelings had become a tool with which to fight western imperialism.

Then there was religion and its response to music. Even the Islamic clerics could not agree as to whether music should be permitted or not. Those who thought it should be allowed also believed that western music was damaging to the principles of a traditional family and tried to keep people away from it. Western music continued to be popular among young people, but there were no opportunities for them to reproduce it or experience it in any way. Although most Iranian families listened to different forms of music, whether it was American pop songs or alternative music, the idea of their own children making such music didn't seem right. Many of the middle-class intellectual families who taught their children to play a classical instrument, such as the violin or piano, were suspicious of rock music and the style of clothing and laid-back lifestyle that went with it.

For girls interested in rock music there were even more restrictions. The idea of a female musician was unthinkable. In the male-oriented society of Iran, a woman is protected by her male relatives, first her father and brother and later her husband. This tradition goes back a long way, long before the Islamic revolution. Women are seen as vulnerable members of society, as well as representing the moral values of the family. So images of women with distinctive looks and movements not considered 'suitable' for a young lady do not fit well.

But regardless of gender, the family became many young people's first experience of censorship. If they wanted to play music, chances are they would be stopped if their family was religious, on the grounds of morality, or if they came from an intellectual family, where music was considered just a hobby and where children were pushed to study to become doctors and lawyers rather than join a band. From music being censored at home it was a short step for an authoritarian government to ban music, even though their reasons might be different – the authorities' main concern was to stop the importation of western culture, but they were also able to exploit Iranian society's own religious and moral standards to enforce that ban. This political stance against a particular kind of music often leads to music and musicians unwittingly becoming part of a political opposition and therefore banned.

Since the 90s, the internet has come to the rescue of young Iranian musicians isolated within their own homes as well as in wider society. While parents, and in general the older generation, did not have enough time to explore this new tool because of their financial responsibilities, younger Iranians took the time to explore and learn to use the internet. Now, when they closed the doors to their bedrooms, they opened the doors to chat rooms instead. Connecting with friends, even of the opposite sex, which was taboo in the outside world, became as easy as talking to your classmates at school.

It also opened the door to discovering other nations, many of them considered 'evil' by the government. The internet created a space for the young

Negar Shaghaghi's band Take It Easy Hospital as featured in No One Knows About Persian Cats, *2009*
Credit: Everett Collections/Rex Features

to discover and judge for themselves, regardless of what was being promoted in the global media, where Iran and the west competed to demonise each other. People communicated with each other beyond the reach of politicians. Young Iranians got to know about more stable societies and discovered the joy of participation in the arts, including music. Music archives expanded in a short time, articles were read about the history of music and the knowledge of the younger generation of Iran expanded, while the gap between them and the older generation widened.

Musicians found each other and bands were formed. In the male-oriented society of Iran, women also decided to step forward and take part. The alienated young rushed to join this underground culture and experience music, and the demand for musical instruments rose in a society where importing a western instrument was a difficult task. In a short period of economic stability in Iran, during the presidency of Mohammad Khatami in the late 90s and early noughties, Iran's middle-class benefited from newfound attention and music had fertile soil to grow in. It was at that time that the first Iranian rock bands, such as Barad, Ohum and 127, were formed and later inspired a younger generation. While Ohum and Barad used the ancient poetry of Iran in their songs, 127 used street language and sang about daily life.

This growing underground music scene led to the building of the first underground studios, with soundproofed rooms and recording equipment. Soon albums were being produced and advertised through the internet, copied onto CDs and brought into every home and car. Many bands at that time decided to make peace with the government and tried to get permission to publish their music and so create the beginnings of an industry that would not go against society's moral values. Their request was turned down by the authorities, who did not include rock in their categories of legal music, because of English lyrics, western instruments or even a high-speed tempo that could be dance music.

A key event for the relationship of the Iranian authorities with western music took place on 1 August 2007 in Karaj, a suburb of Tehran. An unofficial, open-air rock concert, organised by two young bands, Font and Dative, was planned to take place in a garden that was usually hired out for weddings. About 150 people were expected, but 600 turned up as the news of a rock concert spread by word of mouth. The concert was raided by the riot police as it became so big it could no longer be hidden and led to the organisers being arrested and jailed along with 250 members of the audience.

It was after this concert that the government began to realise the extent of the growth of rock music in the country and so redoubled the pressure on musicians by targeting the underground studios and shutting them down. Iran's older generation had to face the reality that rock music was now part of society. But instead of trying to understand and analyse this new phenomenon, they rejected it, ignoring its artistic, social and

Negar Shaghaghi's playlist

Darde eshgh
O-Hum
Available on iTunes

Ye Mosht Sarbaz
Hich-Kas
Available on YouTube

Dreaming
Free Keys
Available on MySpace

creative merits. They saw it as a negative force, an act of anarchy. The media misleadingly associated rock music with drugs and labelled musicians as Satanists. In their reporting of the raided rock concert, it was claimed that the musicians had served blood and screened pornography.

Many concerned parents prohibited their children from participating in music to keep them away from drugs. At the same time, the generation that had passionately played rock was getting close to their 30s – the only thing left of the whole experience was music archives and a few instruments. Many of them were put under pressure to find 'real' jobs and had to abandon their dreams of playing music in order to support families of their own. For a young Iranian, being in a band could never become a career, because no such thing as a music industry existed. In Turkey, however, which is also a Muslim country, companies such as Sony had started to invest in rock, pop and alternative music, which brought Turkey's musicians into the global music scene.

Meanwhile in Iran, the musicians who were forced into office jobs became mentors of younger musicians. The new generation, in turn, who had used the internet from a very young age, took music to a whole new level in terms of musicality and production because they felt the need to become part of the global music community. Their dream was not only to play music, but also to play music to a world standard. Through sites such as YouTube and MySpace, Iranian musicians started to improve their skills and taught themselves how to use production and recording tools. Alongside rock musicians, a new generation of hip-hop artists emerged. 'Persian rap' became extremely popular in a very short time.

One of its pioneers was Hich-Kas ('Nobody'), whose songs about poverty, class, social stereotypes and cultural matters became hugely popular. One of the reasons for hip hop's popularity is that it echoes Iran's long tradition of poetry. Also, it can be produced with a minimum of equipment: the right computer software, headphones and a small room are all that is needed, whereas rock music is based on live performance, and therefore harder to keep hidden.

Many people have tried to make the voices of this young generation of modern musicians heard, including Bahman Ghobadi in his 2009 film *No One Knows About Persian Cats*, which showed the underground music scene in Iran and highlighted the hardships that musicians go through. Iranian musicians are also invited to perform overseas, most notably at the underground music festival held in the Netherlands in 2006, which created an opportunity for many Iranian underground bands to perform.

Despite all the efforts of music fans and musicians to make the sound of this generation heard, the political situation, as well as entrenched cultural traditions in the country, make it extremely difficult. The contested presidential elections of June 2009 have increased the pressure. Parts of the music scene came out in support of the opposition and some musicians were forced into exile, shattering a fragile, newly emerging music scene. Because of the way that music is seen in the eyes of the authorities, it became a political act; art that is associated with politics cannot endure because it loses its influence as one political party is replaced by another.

I asked a friend of mine who recently came to the UK from Iran about the bands and what they were doing and if many of them have quit playing music. He laughed and asked me if I had heard of a new punk rock band. I hadn't, but when I checked their MySpace page, I realised that bands are still playing music in Iran as they always have. But the question of when and how they are going to make it to the global market and have an industry of their own remains unanswered. For me, it is still like running barefoot against runners in their new Nike shoes. ❐

©Negar Shaghaghi
39(3): 51/58
DOI: 10.1177/0306422010379806

Negar Shaghaghi was born in Tehran in 1986. She studied architecture at university. She became the lyricist and songwriter of the duo band Take It Easy Hospital, which featured in Bahman Ghobadi's film *No One Knows About Persian Cats*

10) WOMEX

THE WORLD MUSIC EXPO

www.womex.com

Trade Fair
Showcase Festival
Conference
Networking
Film Market
Awards
virtualWOMEX

Copenhagen, Denmark
27–31 October 2010

NOTES FROM UNDERGROUND

Simon Broughton talks to **Maral Afsharian** about the challenges facing a female singer-songwriter in Tehran – from the authorities to band members

'I did an interview with a blogger who asked me "What's the biggest difficulty you have as a female musician in Iran?" and I said "Dealing with guys."' Maral laughs, because actually the problems confronting women singers are considerable, but problems between band members are universal. 'My difficulty isn't *hijab* or Islam, or all those problems they expect, but it's really difficult to deal with boys here because they think they are in control of everything and can decide whatever they want.'

Maral Afsharian is a singer and musician in her mid-20s in Tehran. I first met her in the apartment of one of her band members in December 2008 where they were rehearsing. There were three of them in a group called The Plastic Wave and she performed a song called 'My Clothes on Other Bodies' – a song about the frustration of seeing other people getting the opportunities you've missed. Her keyboard player Saeid Nadjafi wrote the music and Maral wrote the words in English: 'I prefer to sing in English,' she said, 'because I don't think Farsi suits the sound of rock music so well.' She describes her music as 'electronic psychedelic rock' and it comes with grungy guitar. They were all excited because their demo, selected from thousands of submissions, had won them an invitation to perform in the South By South West (SXSW) Festival in Austin, Texas, one of the most important in the world for Indie music.

Although we were several storeys up, in a city-centre tower block, this was very much an 'underground' rehearsal. The 'rehearsal room' had a blanket over the door to muffle the sound – because there are people around who will report unofficial music. There's nothing political or oppositional in Maral's songs, it's simply the style of music the authorities object to.

To release a record or give a public performance in Iran you have to get authorisation from the Ministry of Culture and Islamic Guidance. This is reasonably straightforward for traditional Iranian music, and during the liberalising influence of President Khatami (1997–2005) pop music, pioneered by the hugely popular group Arian, became officially accepted. But styles like rock, rap and heavy metal don't get permitted. Maral hasn't even bothered to apply for permission: 'I didn't waste my time on that because there are so many rules against what I do. First of all I'm a woman so I can't perform in public, except for women-only events; then I sing in English and English is not an approved language for music here; and the other problem is the genre – western music is banned so why should I waste my time applying for permission?'

Since Mahmoud Ahmadinejad assumed the presidency in 2005, there's been a tightening up on the 'underground' scene. Maral was performing in an unofficial concert in a park in Karaj, west of Tehran, in the summer of 2007, which was broken up by the police – her only brush with the authorities. Many of the musicians were imprisoned and Maral was in jail for three days. 'It was Rajaee Shahr prison in Karaj. It's the worst prison in Iran, full of criminals, murderers, drug dealers. When they want to punish someone in Evin prison they send them to Rajaee Shahr,' she says. The following year, in 2008, the pressure increased with a television documentary called *Shock* which equated underground musicians with drug-users and Satanists. 'It was horrifying the way they depicted us,' says Maral, 'but with this situation in Iran, I prefer to be an "underground" singer. Otherwise you have to do cheesy concerts like Arian. But if I was in some other country, of course I'd love a contract with a good label.'

Although she's only performed unofficially in Iran, Maral has given concerts abroad in Tajikistan, Armenia and the United Arab Emirates. The invitation to SXSW was incredibly exciting and potentially a big break. But sadly it wasn't to be. There was no problem from the Iranian authorities but the American Embassy wouldn't give them a visa, saying they

Maral Afsharian rehearsing in Tehran
Credit: Simon Broughton

didn't think they had enough experience at performing. 'It was a bad bad bad experience for me,' Maral fumes. 'Is it really their business to decide whether we have enough experience or not? But I couldn't say anything and we left.'

The Plastic Wave has now broken up following fellow band member Saeid Nadjafi's attempt to take the group on tour with his sister in place of Maral. Rather ironic given the song I'd heard them singing – 'My Clothes on Other Bodies'. That's why Maral says her biggest problem is dealing with guys in Iran.

Iranian women are well educated and active in the workforce, but they are required to conform to a strict dress code, wearing a headscarf (*hijab*) and keeping the body covered. The law in the Islamic Republic also discriminates against women, which must affect the prevailing attitude towards women – something that the lawyer Shirin Ebadi, who won the Nobel Peace Prize in 2003, notes in her autobiography *Iran Awakening*.

The specific restrictions on music won't permit a female soloist (except in front of an all-female audience), although women backing singers are permitted. Apart from strictly limiting performing opportunities for women (and therefore developing a career), it leads to absurd situations like a concert I attended in 2008 where two female singers, accompanied by a mixed band of instrumentalists, were joined by one of the male instrumentalists on vocals – which sounded musically absurd – just so the women couldn't be described as soloists. Some female singers do perform for women-only audiences but others prefer not to, on principle, and only perform outside the country.

The situation has become more tense, of course, since the disputed elections of June 2009 and, following her experiences in 2007, Maral is keen not to antagonise the authorities by performing unofficially. 'There are places I could do it,' she told me on the phone in June 2010, 'but it's risky. If I get arrested it's going to be a big problem, even bigger than before.'

Maral's biggest problem is dealing with guys in Iran

Maral, like thousands the world over, was shocked by the shooting of Neda Agha-Soltan at a demonstration in Tehran on 20 June 2009. A music student herself, Neda has now become an icon of the Green Movement which protested against what it believes were fraudulent elections. Mobile phone footage of Neda dying on the street was flashed around the world. 'The day she was shot, I was out, but when I got back home I saw lots of messages on my Facebook saying someone was shot in the protests. I looked at the video and I couldn't talk. I watched it over and over and over again and I couldn't forget the look in her eyes. I had a guitar beside my desk and I just picked it up and started playing a song and improvised the lyrics. It just came out of my mind while I was watching the video. I couldn't stop it. I wrote the song and recorded it. It happened very automatically after watching the video. It had to come out of me.'

The song 'Neda' was included on an Iranian underground compilation by Bar-Ax (a UK-based organisation supporting alternative Iranian music) and released by *Songlines*, the world music magazine, in April 2010. Is it dangerous to sing a song like that and email it, I wondered? 'Yes it is,' admits Maral. 'I tried not to sing something political and I looked at what happened to her as a girl. She was studying music so I just imagined her as a girl with some vision in her life who wanted to achieve something she was dreaming of, but didn't have the chance. Suddenly she was just stopped in a terrible way. It's not something I would publically perform – it's just very personal for me.'

Maral supports herself by writing for newspapers and magazines about computer gaming and software. Meanwhile, she's writing and recording material as a solo artist for an EP, although until it's finished she's uncertain whether it's going to be trip-hop or electronic rock.

'I really don't like the restrictions here,' Maral admits. 'I'm not enjoying my life here as long as the situation is like this. But I'd rather live here than run away. I try not to do things against the political situation because it doesn't get me anywhere. For some people music is a hobby, but I have to find a way to do it. It's my life.' ❐

© Simon Broughton
39(3): 60/64
DOI: 10.1177/0306422010380178
www.indexoncensorship.org

Simon Broughton is editor-in-chief of *Songlines* magazine (www.songlines.co.uk). The Iranian underground compilation, including Maral's 'Neda', is available from www.bar-ax.com, or from *Songlines* magazine no.67

PRIMACY OF THE EAR

Jazz musician **Gilad Atzmon** was a committed young Zionist until he heard Charlie Parker play: it was the beginning of a political and musical education

One of my closest friends once pointed out to me that only with her Jewish friends does she always know the exact provenance of their mother and father, only with her Jewish acquaintances does she know precisely how their grandparents survived the last great war. It seems that I, too, when I come to telling my own story, follow this classic Jewish narrative structure. I just can't help it. As hard as I have tried, I have apparently failed in getting that Jewishness out of myself.

My grandfather was a charismatic, poetic, veteran Zionist terrorist. A former prominent commander in the right-wing Irgun terror organisation, he had, I must admit, a tremendous influence on me in my early days. He displayed unrelenting hatred towards anything not Jewish. He hated Germans; consequently, he would not allow my dad to buy a German car. He also despised the British for colonising his 'promised land'. (I can only assume that he didn't detest the Brits as much as the Germans, however, as he did allow my father to drive an old Vauxhall Viva.)

He was also pretty cross with the Palestinians for dwelling on the land he was sure belonged to him and his people. Often, he would wonder: 'These

Arabs have so many countries, why do they have to live on the exact same land that was "given" to us by our God?' More than anything, though, my grandfather hated Jewish leftists. (Here it is important to mention that as Jewish leftists have never produced any recognised model of automobile, this specific loathing didn't mature into a conflict of interests between him and my dad.) As a follower of right-wing revisionist Zionist Ze'ev Jabotinsky, my grandfather evidently realised that leftist philosophy, together with any form of Jewish value system, is a contradiction in terms. Being a veteran right-wing terrorist as well as a proud Jewish hawk, he knew very well that tribalism can never live in peace with humanism and universalism. Following his mentor Jabotinsky, he believed in the 'Iron Wall' philosophy, which maintained that no accommodation with the indigenous Arab population was possible; total separation was essential for the successful colonisation of Palestine, whether through strong government or military force. Like Jabotinsky, my grandfather respected Arab people, he had a high opinion of their culture and religion, yet he believed that Arabs in general, and Palestinians in particular, should be confronted fearlessly and fiercely.

Quoting the anthem of Jabotinsky's political movement, my grandpa would often repeat: 'In blood and sweat, we would erect our race from rotten corners and dust.' My grandfather believed in the revival of the pride of the 'Jewish race', and so did I in my very early days. Like my peers, I didn't see the Palestinians around me. They were no doubt there: they fixed my father's car for half the price, they built our houses, they cleaned the mess we left behind, they schlepped boxes in the local food store, but they always disappeared just before sunset and appeared again before dawn. They never socialised with us. We didn't really understand who they were and what they stood for. Supremacy was brewed into our souls, we gazed at the world through racist, chauvinistic binoculars. And we felt no shame about it either.

At 17, I was getting ready for my compulsory military service in the Israel Defence Forces (IDF). Being a well-built teenager fuelled with Zionist spirit, I was due to join an air-force special rescue unit. But then the unexpected happened. On a very late-night jazz programme, I heard Charlie Parker's *Bird with Strings*.

I was knocked out. The music was more organic, poetic, sentimental and *wilder* than anything I had ever heard before. My father used to listen to Bennie Goodman and Artie Shaw, and those two were entertaining – they could certainly play the clarinet – but Bird was a different story altogether. Here was a fierce, libidinal extravaganza of wit and energy. The following morning I skipped school and rushed to Piccadilly Records, Jerusalem's number-one music shop. I found the jazz section and bought every bebop recording they had on the shelves (which probably amounted to two albums). On the bus home, I realised that Parker was actually a black man. It didn't take me by complete surprise, but it was kind of a revelation. In my world, it was only Jews who were associated with anything good. Bird was the beginning of a journey.

At the time, my peers and I were convinced that Jews were indeed the Chosen People. My generation was raised on the magical victory of the Six-Day War. We were totally sure of ourselves. As we were secular, we associated every success with our omnipotent qualities. We didn't believe in divine intervention, we believed in ourselves. We believed that our might originated in our resurrected Hebraic souls and flesh. The Palestinians, for their part, served us obediently, and it didn't seem at the time that this situation was ever going to change. They displayed no real signs of collective resistance. The sporadic so-called 'terror' attacks made us feel righteous, and filled us with eagerness for revenge. But somehow, amidst this orgy of omnipotence, and to my great surprise, I came to realise that the people who excited me most were actually a bunch of black Americans – people who had nothing to do with the Zionist miracle or with my own chauvinist, exclusivist tribe.

The people who excited me most were actually a bunch of black Americans

It wasn't more than two days before I acquired my first saxophone. It's a very easy instrument to get started on – ask Bill Clinton – but learning to play like Bird or Cannonball Adderley seemed an impossible mission. I began to practise day and night, and the more I did, the more I was overwhelmed by the tremendous achievement of that great family of black American musicians I was beginning to know closely. Within a month I learned about Sonny Rollins, Joe Henderson, Hank Mobley, Thelonious Monk, Oscar Peterson and Duke Ellington, and the more I listened the more I realised that my initial Judeo-centric upbringing was somehow totally misleading.

After one month with a saxophone shoved up my mouth, my Zionist enthusiasm disappeared completely. Instead of flying choppers behind enemy lines, I started to fantasise about living in New York, London or Paris.

All I wanted was a chance to listen to the jazz greats play live (it was the late 70s, and many of them were still around).

Nowadays, youngsters who want to play jazz tend to enrol in a music college. It was very different when I was coming up. Those who wanted to play classical music would join a conservatory, but those who wanted to play for the sake of the music itself would stay at home and swing around the clock. There was no jazz education in Israel at that time, and my hometown, Jerusalem, had just a single, tiny jazz club, housed in an old, converted picturesque Turkish bath. Every Friday afternoon it ran a jam session, and for my first two years in jazz, these jams were the essence of my life. I stopped everything else. I just practised day and night and prepared myself for the next 'Friday Jam'. I listened to the music and transcribed some great solos. I practised in my sleep, imagining the chord changes and flying over them. I decided to dedicate my life to jazz, accepting the fact that as a white Israeli my chances of making it to the top were rather slim.

I did not yet realise that my emerging devotion to jazz had overwhelmed my Zionist tendencies, that it was probably then and there that I left Chosenness behind to become an ordinary human being. Years later, I would indeed come to see that jazz had been my escape route. Within months, though, I began to feel less and less connected to my surrounding reality. I saw myself as part of a far broader and greater family, a family of music lovers, admirable people concerned with beauty and spirit rather than land, mammon and occupation.

However, I still had to join the IDF. Though later generations of young Israeli jazz musicians simply escaped the army and fled to the Mecca of jazz, New York, such an option wasn't available for me, a young lad of Zionist origins in Jerusalem. The possibility didn't even occur to me. In July 1981 I joined the Israeli army, but from my first day of service I did my very best to avoid the call of duty – not

Gilad Atzmon's playlist

Laura
Charlie Parker
Decca

Milonga del Angel
Astor Piazzolla
Pangaea

Clarinet Quintet in B minor Op. 115
Johannes Brahms
Boris Rener, Ludwig Quartet
Naxos

because I was a pacifist; nor did I care that much about the Palestinians. I just preferred to be alone with my saxophone.

In June 1982, when the first Israel-Lebanon war broke, I had been a soldier for a year. It didn't take a genius to figure out the truth. I knew our leaders were lying; in fact, every Israeli soldier understood that this was a war of Israeli aggression. Personally, I no longer felt any attachment to the Zionist cause, Israel or the Jewish people. Dying on the Jewish altar didn't appeal to me anymore. Yet, it still wasn't politics or ethics that moved me, but rather my craving to be alone with my new Selmer Paris saxophone. Playing scales at the speed of light seemed to me far more important than killing Arabs in the name of Jewish suffering. Thus, instead of becoming a qualified killer I spent every possible effort trying to join one of the military bands. It took a few months, but I eventually landed safely in the Israeli Air Force Orchestra (IAFO).

The IAFO was uniquely constituted. You could be accepted for being an excellent musician or promising talent, or for being the son of a dead pilot. The fact that I was accepted knowing that my dad was still amongst the living reassured me; for the first time, I considered the possibility that I might possess musical talent.

To my great surprise, none of the orchestra members took the army seriously. We were all concerned with just one thing: our personal musical development. We hated the army, and it didn't take long before I began to hate the very state that maintained it and required a band for it that wouldn't allow me to practise 24/7. When we were called to play for a military event, we would try to play as poorly as we could just to make sure we would never get invited again. Sometimes we even gathered in the afternoon just to *practise* playing badly. We realised that the worse we performed as a collective, the more personal freedom we would gain. In the military orchestra I learned for the first time how to be subversive, how to sabotage the system in order to pursue an immaculate personal ideal.

In the summer of 1984, just three weeks before I shed my military uniform, we were sent to Lebanon for a concert tour. At the time it was a very dangerous place to be. The Israeli army was dug deep in bunkers and trenches, avoiding any confrontation with the local population. On the second day we set out for Ansar, a notorious Israeli internment camp in South Lebanon. This experience was to change my life completely.

At the end of a dusty dirt track on a boiling hot day in early July, we arrived at hell on earth. The huge detention centre was enclosed with barbed

wire. As we drove to the camp headquarters, we had a view of thousands of inmates in the open air being scorched by the sun.

As difficult as it might be to believe, military bands are always treated as VIPs, and once we landed at the officers' barracks we were taken on a guided tour of the camp. We walked along the endless barbed wire and guard towers. I couldn't believe my eyes.

'Who are these people?' I asked the officer.

'Palestinians,' he said. 'On the left are PLO [Palestine Liberation Organisation], and on the right are Ahmed Jibril's boys [Popular Front for the Liberation of Palestine – General Command] – they are far more dangerous, so we keep them isolated.'

I studied the detainees. They looked very different to the Palestinians in Jerusalem. The ones I saw in Ansar were angry. They were not defeated, and they were numerous. As we continued past the barbed wire I gazed at the inmates, and arrived at an unbearable truth: I was walking on the other side, in Israeli military uniform. The place was a concentration camp. The inmates were the 'Jews', and I was nothing but a 'Nazi'. It took me years to realise that even the binary opposition Jew/Nazi was in itself a result of my Zionist indoctrination.

While I contemplated the resonance of my uniform, trying to deal with the great sense of shame growing in me, we came to a large, flat piece of ground at the centre of the camp. The officer guiding us offered more platitudes about the current war to defend our Jewish haven. While he was boring us to death with these irrelevant lies, I noticed that we were surrounded by two dozen concrete blocks, each around one square metre in area and 1.3 metres high, with small metal doors as entrances. I was horrified at the thought that my army was locking guard dogs into these boxes for the night. Putting my Israeli *chutzpah* into action, I confronted the officer about these horrible concrete dog cubes. He was quick to reply: 'These are our solitary confinement blocks; after two days in one of these, you become a devoted Zionist!'

This was enough for me. I realised that my affair with the Israeli state and with Zionism was over. Yet I still knew very little about Palestine, about the *Nakba* (Palestinian term for 1948, the catastrophe) or even about Judaism and Jewishness, for that matter. I only saw then that, as far as I was concerned, Israel was bad news, and I didn't want to have anything further to do with it. Two weeks later I returned my uniform, grabbed my alto sax, took the bus to Ben Gurion Airport and left for Europe for a few months, to busk in the street. At the age of 21, I was free for the first time. However, December proved too cold for me, and I returned home – but with the clear intention to make it back to Europe.

It took another ten years before I could leave Israel for good. During that time, however, I began to learn about the Israel-Palestine conflict, and to accept that I was actually living on someone else's land. I took in the devastating fact that in 1948 the Palestinians hadn't abandoned their homes willingly – as we were told in school – but had been brutally ethnically cleansed by my grandfather and his ilk. I began to realise that ethnic cleansing has never stopped in Israel, but has instead just taken on different forms, and to acknowledge the fact that the Israeli legal system was not impartial but racially orientated (for example, the 'law of return' welcomes Jews 'home' from any country supposedly after 2,000 years, but prevents Palestinians from returning to their villages after two years abroad). All the while, I had also been developing as a musician, becoming a major session player and a musical producer. I wasn't really involved in any political activity, and though I scrutinised the Israeli leftist discourse I soon realised that it was very much a social club rather than an ideological force motivated by ethical awareness.

At the time of the Oslo accords in 1993, I just couldn't take it anymore. I saw that Israeli 'peacemaking' was nothing but spin. Its purpose wasn't to reconcile with the Palestinians or confront Zionist original sin, but to further secure the existence of the Jewish State at the expense of the Palestinians. For the Israelis, *shalom* doesn't mean 'peace': it means security, and for Jews only. A Palestinian law of return wasn't an option. I decided to leave my home and my career. I left everything and everyone behind, including my wife Tali, who joined me later. All I took with me was my tenor saxophone – my true, eternal friend.

For the Israelis, shalom doesn't mean peace: it means security

I moved to London and began postgraduate studies in philosophy at the University of Essex. Within a week, I managed to obtain a residency at the Black Lion, a legendary Irish pub in the Kilburn High Road. At the time

I failed to appreciate how lucky I was: I didn't know how difficult it was to get a gig in London. In fact, this was the beginning of my international career as a jazz musician. Within a year I had become very popular in the UK, playing bebop and post-bop. Within three years I was playing with my band all over Europe.

Yet it didn't take long before I began to feel homesick. To my great surprise, however, it wasn't Israel I missed; not Tel Aviv, not Haifa, not Jerusalem. It was *Palestine*. It wasn't rude taxi drivers at Ben Gurion Airport, or shopping centres in Ramat Gan, but the little place in Yefet Street, Jaffa, that served great hummus, and the Palestinian villages stretched across the hills amidst olive trees and *sabra* cacti. Whenever I fancied a visit home, in London, I would end up in the Edgware Road, spending the evening at a Lebanese restaurant. Once I started to fully express my thoughts about Israel in public, it soon became clear to me that Edgware Road was probably as close as I could ever get to my homeland.

When I lived in Israel, admittedly, I hadn't been at all taken with Arab music (supremacist colonials are rarely interested in the indigenous culture). I loved folk music and had already established myself in Europe as a klezmer player, and over the years I had begun playing Turkish and Greek music as well. Yet I had completely skipped over Arab music – and Palestinian music in particular. In London, hanging out in those Lebanese restaurants, it began to occur to me that I had never really explored the music of my neighbours. More worrisomely, I had ignored and even dismissed it. Though it had been all around me, I had never really *listened* to it. It had been there at every corner of my life: the call to prayer from the mosques, the voices of Umm Kulthum, Farid el Atrash and Abdel Halim Hafez. It could be heard in the streets, on television, in the small cafes in Jerusalem's Old City, in the restaurants. It had been all around me – but I had, disrespectfully, never given it any notice.

In my mid-30s, away from the Middle East, I became drawn to the indigenous music of my homeland. It wasn't easy; it was, in fact, on the verge of being completely unfeasible. As much as jazz was easy for me to absorb, Arab music was almost impossible. I would put the music on, grab my saxophone or clarinet, try to integrate my sound with it and come out sounding utterly foreign. I soon realised that Arab music was a completely different language altogether. I didn't know where to start, or how to approach it.

To a certain extent, jazz music is a western product with an extensive Afro-Cuban influence. It evolved at the beginning of the 20th century and developed at the margins of American culture. Bebop, the music I grew up on, consists of relatively short fragments of music. The tunes are short because they had to fit into the three-minute record format of the 1940s. Western music can be easily transcribed into some visual content via standard notation and chord symbols. Jazz, like most western musical forms, is therefore partially digital. Arab music, on the other hand, is analogue – it cannot be transcribed. Its authenticity evaporates in the attempt. By the time I achieved enough humane maturity to literally face the music of my homeland, my musical knowledge stood in the way.

I couldn't understand what it was that stopped me from encompassing Arab music, or why it didn't sound right when I tried to play it. I had spent enough time listening and practising, but it just didn't work. As time went by, European music journalists began to appreciate my new sound and to regard me as a new jazz 'hero' who crossed the divide as an expert in Arab music. I knew they were wrong, though, much as I had indeed tried to cross this so-called 'divide'. I could easily tell that my sound and interpretation were foreign to true Arab music.

Then I discovered an easy trick. During my concerts, when trying to emulate this elusive Oriental sound, I would first sing a line that reminded me of the sounds I had ignored in my childhood. I would try to recall the echoing call of the *muezzin* sneaking its way into our streets from the surrounding valleys, and the astonishing, haunting sounds of my friends Dhafer Youssef and Nizar al Issa, as well as the low, lingering voice of Abdel Halim Hafez. Initially, I would just close my eyes and listen with my internal ear, but without realising it I began to open my mouth gradually as well, and to sing loudly. Then I realised that if I sang with the saxophone in my mouth, I would arrive at a sound that closely approximated the mosques' metal horns. I had tried to draw closer to the Arab sound for so long, but now I simply forgot what I was trying to achieve and began to enjoy myself.

After a while I noticed that the echoes of Jenin, al Quds (Jerusalem) and Ramallah began to emerge naturally from the bell of my saxophone. I asked myself what had happened, why it suddenly sounded genuine, and concluded that I had given up on the primacy of the eye and devoted my attention instead to the primacy of the ear. I didn't look for inspiration on the page, for the visual or the forensic, in musical notation or chord symbols. Instead, I listened to my internal voice. Struggling with Arab music reminded me why I had begun to play music in the first place. After all, I had heard Bird on the radio; I did not see him on MTV.

Through music, and particularly my very personal struggle with Arab music, I learned to *listen*. Rather than looking at history or analysing its evolution in material terms, it is listening that stands at the core of deep comprehension. Ethical behaviour comes into play when the eyes are shut and the echoes of conscience can form a tune within one's soul. To empathise is to accept the primacy of the ear. ❏

©Gilad Atzmon
39(3): 66/77
DOI: 10.1177/0306422010379690
www.indexoncensorship.org

Gilad Atzmon's latest album is *In Loving Memory of America* (Enja). He performs with the Orient House Ensemble and is the author of two novels, *Guide to the Perplexed* (Serpent's Tail) and *My One and Only Love* (Saqi Books)

WORDSANDMUSIC

Malu Halasa on
Chuy y Mauricio/El Potro de Sinaloa

In the Humaya cemetery in the Mexican state of Sinaloa, tastefully designed colonial styled, multi-storey mausoleums, some with running water and air-con, are testimonies to the fallen heroes in America's war against drugs. In death, as in life, the illicit drugs trade has seeped into all aspects of Mexican culture, no more so than in the country's popular tradition of romantic outlaw ballads. 'Chuy y Mauricio' by the romantic singer El Potro de Sinaloa ('The Colt of Sinaloa'), José Hernandez, released in 2007, is a *narcocorrido,* part of a living folk tradition with a modern brutal edge.

Performed by trumpets, trombones, tubas, clarinets and drums, this infectious polka from northern Mexico tells the story of the murder of two drug traffickers in Sinaloa. Chuy and Mauricio have 400 pounds of *mota* (Mexico City slang for marijuana) and a fast get-away car, a Chrysler 300. The song has inspired a successful low-budget, domestically produced, violent *narcocinema* film, with sequels, aptly titled *El Chrysler 300*. Other singers have recorded 'Chuy y Mauricio' but it is El Potro de Sinaloa's rendition, with an accompanying karaoke video on YouTube, that nearly 100,000 people have sung along to.

For over a hundred years, *corridos* have related the exploits of brave men and women who died fighting the authorities – revolutionaries, cross-border smugglers, *tequileros* (bootleggers during Prohibition) and desperados. In the 70s, dead drug dealers became the subject of songs, but as trade grew exponentially, with coke and heroin from South America and cannabis and, more recently, methamphetamine from Mexico, an explosion of singers and songs since the 90s have reflected a shift in song content. With more living cartel members wanting their exploits bigged-up in popular ballads, *narco-corridos* started including the wider drug trade – its codes and trophies like the Chrysler 300 in 'Chuy y Mauricio'.

In the beginning, the song's two protagonists are 'felices y muy contentos' (happy and contented). Their 400-weight was probably locally grown and harvested in one of the hideaway farms in Sinaloa's serrated, straggling Sierra Madre Occidental mountain range. The men would have gone on their merry way, if not for a cruel trick of fate ('Que jugada del Destino') that takes them in the opposite direction to 'Contrario'.

Flash cars can attract unwanted attention, and Chuy and Mauricio make a fatal mistake of picking up 'la Muerte' (Death) who, in the back seat, figures out a way of stealing their money. The lyrics do not reveal what kind of weapon she used but things happen quickly: Chuy falls dead in the passenger seat on the right and Mauricio on the driver's side. Their fictional deaths join the 20,000 real ones of people who have been killed in Mexico's drug-related violence over the past four years.

The next verse in the song tells the aftermath of the murders: more tombs in the beautiful colonial town of San Ignacio, and more families crying. Chuy and Mauricio were fans of the group Los Canelos de Durango, particularly their *narcocorrido* 'Vida Mafiosa' (Gangster Life), a record their friends and family play in their honour one last time.

The song ends with a traditional Spanish farewell – the *despedida*: 'Rancho el chilar Sinaloa ya no volverás a verlos ...' (Rancho el chilar Sinaloa, you will never see them again ...). This 'rancho' is not a reference to the ranches or drug plantations glorified in other *narcocorridos* where goat, *chiva*, is slang for heroin. It is Chuy's and Mauricio's manor, their stomping ground – hot chilli Sinaloa – that will never see them again.

Narcocorridos have been banned from radio in all the Mexican states along the US border. 'The people who are doing these songs have no objection to the ban. Universally they think it's good for business,' explains Elijah Wald, author of *Narcocorrido: A Journey into the Music of Guns, Drugs and Guerrillas*.

The murders of narcosingers and musicians, including the gangland slayings of singer Sergio Vega in June and La Gallo de Ora ('The Golden Rooster') Valentin Elizade in 2006, have not in fact reached the sensational numbers reported by the US press. For Wald, the arrest of *norteño* accordion-player Roman Ayala at the party for the Beltrán Leyva Cartel in December confirms the insidious relationship between popular music and the cartels. A Mexican congressman has proposed prosecuting anyone selling videos or CDs glorifying the drug trade. 'A nonstarter,' believes Wald, who cites a line from the song 'Pacas de a kilo' (Packets of Cocaine) by the best-selling Los Tigres del Norte: 'Los piños me dan la sombra'

(The pines give me shade). 'The pines' is another name for the Mexican White House.

With its rollicking oom-pa-pa rhythms and snazzy horn breaks, 'Chuy y Mauricio' encloses a bitter valentine. In the macho world of romantic *narcocorridos*, the bad men of the Mexican drug cartels have feelings too. ❒

©Malu Halasa
39(3): 78/80
DOI: 10.1177/0306422010379802
www.indexoncensorship.org

Malu Halasa is an author, editor and journalist. Her books include *Transit Tehran* (Garnet) and *The Secret Life of Syrian Lingerie* (Chronicle). She was one of the foremost journalists writing about rap for the British music press in the 1980s

ROUGH TRADE

ough Trade Multi Million pound Conglomerate
ish to announce that they are still trading
n the best records that can be found as well
s the hardest hard core sounds of the new wave.

nyoneeinterested in acquiring these records
s a mail order customer or from the shops....

lease visit us at:

ww.roughtrade.com

r

1, Brick Lane, London E1 6QL
hone 020 - 7392 - 7788

nd

30, Talbot Road, London W11 1JA
hone 020 - 7229 - 8541

emember: This is still the organisation that
oesn't give a damn about Joe Public.

DISPATCHES FROM A NEW GENERATION

Musician **Khyam Allami** thought the Middle East music scene was in decline, until he went on a personal quest and encountered the new talent of the region

Over the past couple of years, I've been fortunate enough to travel to the Arab world to study music, take a look at the independent music scene and find out what a new generation of musicians are up to. I was born to Iraqi parents in Damascus and moved to London in 1990 when I was nine years old, so my relationship with the Arab world has always been vicarious, seen through the eyes of an older generation. My family's social circle of journalists, writers, painters, musicians and poets were exiles, some of them unable to rebuild what they saw as demolished or to continue the struggle. If it wasn't stories of nostalgia I heard, it was black-humoured accounts of one war or another, politics, petty squabbles or a sad tone of resignation at what they had lost, especially with regards to the music of their era. Nothing is, or could ever be, as good as it was.

Although this gave me an insight into the depth of Arab culture, and what it had achieved over 40 years ago, it was all centred on the past. I would always ask myself: could it be possible that the Arab world stopped producing anything of cultural value since the late 70s? It seemed that a rich, vibrant and powerful music had degenerated into a culturally inferior, mass-produced variation of the same product, sold through a 21st-century media bazaar that thinks it's moving with the times because it uses video clips.

The decades stretching from the 40s to the late 70s gave rise to a vibrant, productive and prosperous period Even though this was an era of revolution and war, it was during this time that oil production, investment, nationalisation and the media started to grow. Arts and culture flourished with the expansion of radio, television and cinema. This gave rise to creativity and inspiration, particularly in Cairo, which became the musical centre of the Arab world. These developments reached their peak during the 60s and 70s, which is why those decades are often regarded as golden years. Sadly, from that point onwards, continuous political upheavals, war and the grip of dictatorial regimes took hold. In turn, culture and the arts slowly began to suffer, descending from inspiring heights to slumber throughout the 80s across the region.

I spent many years listening to all kinds of alternative rock and metal, and playing bass and drums in various independent bands. The DIY independent music scene in Europe and America was a huge influence on me. I then took up the oud ('ūd, Middle Eastern lute) in 2004 and started a BA in ethnomusicology at the School of Oriental and African Studies, University of London, the following year. Through these studies I slowly became more intimate with the music of the entire Middle East, especially the Arab world and Iraq in particular.

By studying this music from the more classical perspective, I felt that I was engaging with a past that is no longer relevant. According to what I could see and hear, everything good had apparently vanished by the end of the 70s. Since then it had been nothing but synthesiser-based pop that took over the airwaves, the television and more recently the mobile phone. Not having any direct contact with the region, Google became my only window.

When I started hunting on the internet for a different kind of Arabic music, something that the new generation was doing, I had much difficulty. Not knowing where to start or even what to look for didn't help, but it was impossible to find anything. After discovering nothing but some ensembles doing the standard instrumental Arabic repertoire and a couple of minor rock bands doing bad covers of the Egyptian diva Um Kulthum, I was disappointed. Was there no independent music going on in the Arab world? Or was it just proving impossible to find?

From my perspective, apart from traditional music released by labels such as Ocora or Network Medien and the Iraqi oud virtuoso Naseer Shamma, in particular his album *Hilal* with his ensemble Oyoun, it all seemed a little

Khyam Allami (right) and Hazem Shaheen
Credit: Yasmine el Baramawy

dry. Dismayed, I continued studying the oldies rigorously and commenced another round of searching a couple of years ago. Finally ... jackpot! I stumbled on the record labels Incognito and Forward Music, both based in Beirut, and Eka3, which has bases in Cairo, Beirut and Amman. Needless to say, I felt like an idiot for coming across them so late, but at least I had found them. It was a revelation. There are young people in the Arab world who play something other than the conservatoire-led classical music, who don't listen to or play commercial pop music, and there are some labels spreading the word. Arabic music is not limited to the golden era of the 60s and 70s or re-issues of traditional music by major European record labels.

Eka3: breaking the mould

Eka3 is one of the Arab world's youngest up-and-coming independent record labels. Founded in 2007 by Tamer Abu Ghazaleh, a creative musician and performer in his own right based in Amman, it has spent the last three years

Rotana: queen of the music scene

Watching the main Arabic TV stations, MTV Arabia or any of the channels provided by the commercial music giant Rotana, leaves you with the clear impression that the population of the Arab world, especially the younger generation, thrives on nothing but commercial songs mass marketed by the media. For those a little older, there remains a nostalgia for the golden classics of Mohammad Abdel Wahab, Um Kulthum, Fairuz or Abdel Halim Hafez. The majority of the stars who sing these commercial pop songs are signed to the Rotana record label. Their songs are owned by Rotana. They are recorded and produced by Rotana. Their videos are produced by Rotana. Their CDs and cassettes are manufactured and distributed by Rotana. And in every shop, cafe or restaurant, the TV will most likely be set to either one of the many 24-hour news broadcasters or one of Rotana's music TV channels. Owned by Saudi billionaire Prince al Waleed bin Talal, the nephew of the Saudi King Abdullah, Rotana is a huge pan-Arab media conglomerate which includes TV stations, radio stations, a film production company, a magazine and Rotana records which has more than 100 major artists on its roster. On its Facebook page, which at the time of writing has 59,165 people who 'like' it, Rotana describes itself as 'the largest Arabic content producer and media company in the world'.

In a video interview with Steve Forbes on the Forbes website published in January 2010 (http://www.forbes.com/2010/01/23/pandit-citi-honeymoon-intelligent-investing-alwaleed_2.html), Prince al Waleed bin Talal spoke about his media holdings and Rotana stating, 'We are the second biggest shareholder, after the Murdoch family, in News Corp, and we have smaller stakes in Disney and Time Warner and we are partners with Disney and Euro Disney in Paris. And yes, we do have a big media company in the Arab world that covers all the main region, the Middle East/North Africa region. And we have around 45 per cent of all the movies and we have around 80 per cent of all the music there and we are using technology to advance our causes there. We have some magazine [sic], we have some cafes. So, yes, we're a very dominant force in the music and the movie industry in the Arab world through Rotana.'

The TV stations owned and run by Rotana include Rotana Cinema (new films), Rotana Clip (music videos), Rotana Mousica (music) and Rotana Zaman (old films and music). It also has a religious channel called al Resalah (The Message). All of these channels are available for streaming on Rotana's website, alongside music by its many artists, for free. Rotana also has a phenomenal distribution network covering almost every single CD or cassette stockist in the Arab world. From the large Virgin megastores to the very small local music shops and the tiniest of kiosks that sell snacks, cold soft drinks and cigarettes on street corners. **KA**

fervently supporting and nurturing the independent music scene across the region. Rather than confining itself to one city, Eka3 has bases in Cairo, Beirut and Amman. Its six-member team (two in each city) checks on how releases are doing and organises events by dealing directly with artists, theatres, venues, shops and the public.

'From the beginning, the project was intended to be regional', explains Tamer Abu Ghazaleh. 'We didn't start from a single place because I knew for a fact that the real problem, for me as an artist, was to find a way of giving the region the necessary exposure. I could be living in Cairo or Amman and distribute my album myself, but that wasn't the requirement. The requirement was that I could create music, with channels ready to take this music, rather than having to think every time, what can I do with this album, who do I give it to, how will it be distributed? It was a headache.'

The last three years for Eka3 have been an uphill struggle, consisting of a series of different initiatives all based on trial and error, especially when it came to distribution, which has proved to be the most difficult task. 'We know we are catering to a niche market that doesn't go to all the shops and areas in a city. They go to particular cafes, theatres, cultural centres, bookshops and even accessory shops. We made an effort to go directly to those places and ask them to stock our releases because we felt that their customers would be interested.'

But when dealing with the more *shabi* (popular) neighbourhoods that don't necessarily form part of their niche he remarked: 'Those were a little difficult. Either they didn't sell or you find out that the owner lost the CD stand with all the albums, or he's taken it into storage and we then find it covered in dust as if it had been buried. It didn't really work out.' These neighbourhoods are a prime target for Rotana, a company that dominates the music industry in the Middle East. Rotana's artists are regularly on television, radio and in the press, whilst Eka3 musicians are on the fringes.

This has only encouraged Tamer and his team to try different approaches including direct marketing. 'For now we're trying to expand our niche market to the maximum possible and the next step will be to take specific releases to specific places. For example, music that might be more appealing to a mass audience, we will take those releases to the more *shabi* areas to see how it goes. The more oriental music we'll take to the music institutes, the jazz artists to jazz bars.'

But what about releasing this music in the first place? All the countries in the region require that any CD, cassette, DVD or music video that is released or sent to television and radio must have permission from the state. Copies of the works must be sent to censorship committees and get approval before they are allowed to be sold or broadcast anywhere. Overall, this hasn't affected the label's work too much, but an incident recently caused it to lose an entire pressing of CDs because of a song that mentioned the name Susan.

What's in a name?

Eka3 is now working with the Jordanian Yazan al Rousan and his group Autostrad. Over the last few years, Yazan's popularity has been on the rise. There is little Arabic influence on his music, but he resonates lyrically with the younger generation, through his perspective and commentary. His new album includes a love song 'Alf Tahieh' (A Thousand Greetings) about a girl named Susan. Earlier this year, the Egyptian government refused permission for its release: President Hosni Mubarak's wife also shares the first name Susan, and the Egyptian censorship committee didn't want listeners to think that Yazan was referring to her. The same process of obtaining permission applies in all the other countries of the region, with some far more restrictive than others. Lebanon is relatively trouble-free as long as you don't seriously offend anybody, while Saudi Arabia, for example, doesn't allow any depiction of humans on the artwork of CDs.

'It has become a given for artists that they can't go out of this frame because the work will be refused and no one will hear it,' comments Tamer. 'There are many artists who produce amazing work, but to a large extent if it breaks anything, it breaks the framework of Arabic music. And I think it's because we are raised to believe that you can break the rules in this particular space [music] and no one will really understand and there are no censors who can judge you. If a work breaks certain rules and the censors say "No", then we'll have something to say to them. But right now we have nothing to say to them and none of the artists want to be refused in any way.' Was it because of the risk? 'It's a risk, yes, but for who? With regards to the artists, what can happen to them? Be put in prison? The maximum that can happen is that the product will lose money. And this is a risk that we [Eka3] are willing to take, as long as there is something being said, that it's not just breaking the rules for the sake of it. If it's art, it's art.'

It's a view shared by the young Amman-based Palestinian journalist and music critic Ahmad Zatari, who observes that the Jordanian government is now using hip-hop artists in its anti-drugs campaign. 'There is a retreat in everything, not just music. If we want to hold the Arab world to account, the position that should be taken so as to lead this change should be taken in the first instance by the *muthaqqafin*, the intellectuals. These people retreated for many reasons, some because their governments "bought" them. In Jordan, for example, there has been an effort over the last 50 or 60 years to calm any action amongst the intellectuals, from the inside. It's for this reason that you don't hear of a single well-known Jordanian writer, intellectual or thinker.

'This has had an effect on the musical movement. There is much creative output from musicians on an artistic level, even new genres are being created and this movement is likely to be influential and comparable with the works of any Lebanese or Egyptian musicians, but we don't have the culture of revolution and by that I don't mean revolutionary like the French students in 68, I mean it in the lighter sense, that of change.'

Forward Music: a lesson in eloquence

Forward Music is based in Beirut, a city that has always been a creative hub for artists, despite its tumultuous past. The label was co-founded in 2001 by the musician and producer Ghazi Abdel Baki. Its artists are as diverse as the city of Beirut, featuring many genres from traditional or classical Arabic music to various kinds of fusion and contemporary musical excursions. With strong independent distribution in the Arab world and Europe, it has been a successful venture and plays a vital role in nurturing and presenting independent artists to the audiences of the Middle East and beyond. It has also recently taken over the distribution of some of Incognito's artists, a rival label founded in 2004 that has recently wound down its activities. Due to Forward Music's hard work, the popularity of its artists and the support of

Culture of complaint

On 23 May, Cairo gave birth to Koral Shakawa al Qahira, the Cairo Complaints Choir, at the Townhouse Gallery – a renowned independent cultural centre. The Complaints Choir was a project conceived in Helsinki by two Finnish artists, Tellervo Kalleinen and Oliver Kochta-Kallleinen, in 2005. Since then, more than 65 Complaints Choirs have been independently created across the world, with Cairo the most recent addition.

The choir's performance launched an exhibition called 'Invisible Publics'. The 23-member choir composed the lyrics, music and learnt four original songs in a week. Shortly after the premier, a number of articles appeared in the English-language online Egyptian press, such as *The Daily Star Egypt*, and a video of their performance was posted on YouTube (http://www.youtube.com/watch?v=U1r_mSUyP2w). Taking their inspiration from all that there is to complain about in their smoggy metropolis, the Cairo Complaints Choir presented their complaints in Egyptian dialect, going through Cairo's problems one by one. To the sound of the oud, melodica and percussion, the first few lines extol the virtues of the 'Europe 2000' who were brought in 'to clean up Cairo's streets, but they just made them bigger garbage heaps'. This was succinctly followed by a comment about the paradoxical sheikh who appears on TV just to tell the viewer that TV is *haram* (impermissible).

As the song begins to pick up its tempo, we hear a repeated refrain set to two notes: 'The workers are not listened to, even the factories have been sold. The wheat [we eat] is American and they are sending our gas abroad.' While keeping the song's tempo steady, the choir begin a decrescendo until they are almost whispering. Hovering above the continuous refrain, a single male voice enters with a *mawal* (improvised sung poetry), beautifully improvising the following verse in the minor *maqam* (mode) *nahawand*: 'Be careful calling our gas natural or they'll say you don't understand. Our gas is now known as normalised gas, sold at a loss, with no remorse.' To a rowdy applause of appreciation, the choir begins its crescendo and at its peak takes off with the lines:

'I am a stranger in my own country, my rights are trampled on. Banks instead of gardens, all sense of justice gone.'

I spoke to Shadi el Hosseini, the choir's melodica player and one of the Eka3 record label's Cairo-based operatives, on Skype. He told me that the day after the performance Egypt's intelligence services made a trip to the Townhouse gallery and a few phone calls to the Dutch embassy, who partly financially supported the 'Invisible Publics' exhibition. They were concerned that there was some kind of foreign influence behind the project, since the choir was created by two Finnish artists.

Due to some justified concern at the Townhouse, the choir is now unable to continue working there, with no hard feelings. Regardless, however, they are planning to continue to develop their project. 'There were many people who saw the show and many who saw the video on YouTube, over 1200 viewings, and as a result some people in Cairo's Shubra quarter are now making plans to launch their own choir.'

'This is what we want, the culture of complaint, which is also linked to people protesting and refusing any type of police violence, it's that spirit that we want to communicate. If you have a problem, if something is bothering you, complain. It's your right to complain in front of people, not just to whisper it in your friend's ear whilst sitting in a cafe, afraid in case there is someone from the *mukhabarat* (intelligence services) next to you listening in. This is your right. And if we present this idea through song, it might just help.' **KA**

the Lebanese media, it has managed to build a wide and varied fan base across the region. It has grown from being a few hard-working friends into a large network of artists and musicians working towards a common goal. During my conversation with Ghazi, I asked him if they had encountered any problems with the release or distribution of their albums. 'One good thing about Lebanon is the variety and diversity of people here. Although it creates a lot of problems at times, it allows you to have some leeway in the margin of expression that doesn't necessarily exist in other places. We haven't had any issues so far, with anyone, regarding the content of the music itself. But I must say that we do practise some kind of restraint. I don't want to say we're censoring ourselves, but rather to say what we need to say in the most elegant way. We don't need to be crude and in your face. I'm sure that even if we had that in our albums it wouldn't be a problem but we try to maintain a certain eloquence.'

Piracy rules: Syrian style

For independent artists to have any kind of presence in Damascus and other Syrian cities, they have to perform live and most of them have almost disregarded the notion of recording out of necessity rather than choice. The main reason for this state of affairs is CD piracy. Copyright laws do exist in Syria, yet no one from the public, the vendors or official bodies takes any notice. CDs are copied and sold in the many independent CD shops across the city at low prices. This has created a market in which it is impossible to sell an original copy of any release unless it's at a loss. And who wants to sell their albums without the prospect of breaking even? This piracy, alongside illegal filesharing, has also affected the Saudi music giant Rotana greatly. According to Tamer Abu Ghazaleh from Eka3, it has forced Rotana to bring CD prices down from around $12 USD to around $5 USD across the region. Rotana claims that it was a strategic decision. An independent small music shop owner in Damascus broke down the average prices for me: an original CD in Damascus is sold for around 200 Syrian pounds, roughly £2.78 GBP or €3.37 EUR; a copied or pirated CD is sold for 25 Syrian pounds, roughly £0.34 GBP or €0.42 EUR, and sometimes even 15 Syrian pounds.

For this reason, almost all musicians in Damascus must perform live as much as possible to gain any exposure. Since both Facebook and YouTube are blocked by the Syrian government, it is impossible for them to utilise the internet in the same way as other artists across the globe. But this hasn't deterred them. A CD compilation produced by Incognito and its Syrian sister-company Majal, titled *The New Oriental Sounds,* featured nine tracks by seven different independent Syrian groups of various genres and styles including Hewar, Lena Chamamyan and Basel Rajoub and

Khyam Allami's playlist

7ob (Love)
Tamer Abu Ghazaleh
Eka3

Problem
Hazem Shaheen
Incognito

Salma Ya Salma
Issa Ghandour and the Madina Band
Forward Music

Album cover for Ghazi Abdel Baki's The Last Communiqué,
Forward Music, December 2009

Itar Shameh. The CD compilation was distributed free in an attempt to shine a light on local alternative bands and artists. Despite Incognito's brave attempt to create a legitimate market neither Eka3 nor Forward Music have followed their example yet.

Postcards of our times

Despite the difficulties, the entire region is witnessing positive change. Many artists have started to express their dissatisfaction through musical developments which are subtle in their references and eloquent in their execution. This in turn is rebuilding the foundations of a rich musical past and leaving a clear path for others to follow. Artists such as Hazem Shaheen or Mustafa Said are clearly Egyptian in their musical voices, no matter how experimental they attempt to be. The same can be said of Yazan al Rousan's Jordanian background. Yet none of these artists express any kind of nationalistic sentiment in any of their work; they are well aware of their influences and the shared cultural heritage across the region, but they are

The maestros of Egypt

In February 2009, I travelled to Cairo, on a research trip for my Masters funded by the British Institute for the Study of Iraq. I spent more than three months studying with the Iraqi oud virtuoso Naseer Shamma at his *Beit ul 'Ūd al 'Arabi* (Arab Oud House), with the legendary Egyptian violinist and composer Abdo Dagher at his home, and at the Cairo Opera House with Hazem Shaheen, a phenomenal oud player who released an album on Incognito records with his group Masar. Upon hearing the first few bars of oud, piano, double bass and percussion on 'Zay El Moga', the opening track of Masar's 2006 debut album *El Aysh wel Melh*, I was hooked. Such a seamless fusion of styles, intelligent and sensitive. I won't continue by raving on about the beauty and vision in Hazem's second album, *Hagat Wahshani* (Things That I Miss), released last year also on Incognito records. Then there was the music of Mustafa Said, an Egyptian oud player, singer and composer, currently residing in Beirut and teaching at Antonine University. His settings of the Arabic translations of Omar Khayyam's 'Rubaiyat' by the Iraqi poet Ahmad Safi al Najjafi (set to music for the first time) and released on Beirut's Forward Music label, breathe new life into what is often regarded as music that belongs to wax cylinders and 78rpm records in the annals of dusty libraries.

Hazem Shaheen has become a highly admired figure amongst the community of young Egyptian musicians. His group Eskenderella performs the songs of many Arabic artists including a few of their own compositions. But most of their repertoire focuses on the following artists: Sayyed Darwish (who died in 1923), the renowned innovator of Egyptian and Arabic music whose operettas captured the true feelings of Cairo's working class in the early 20th century; Sheikh Imam (who died in 1995), who set to music and sang the poetry of his contemporary Ahmad Fouad Negm; and the Lebanese jazz pianist, composer/songwriter and playwright Ziad Rahbani (son of Fairuz, the queen of Lebanese song). Since Eskenderella's first concerts back in 2005, they have seen their audience grow and change, with more and more of the young generation becoming fans. Having kept in touch with

Hazem, I called to interview him via telephone from London shortly after an Eskenderella rehearsal in Cairo. Sheikh Imam was a regular visitor to Hazem's home when he was growing up. 'Sayyed Darwish is our teacher, he is the god of music in Egypt, nobody could ever reach the same level as him. What I, and all of us, have learnt from Sayyed Darwish and Sheikh Imam is to respect the minds and feelings of the listeners.' Eskenderella's first shows had a generally poor attendance, but as soon as they printed on their flyers and posters that they would perform the songs of Sayyed Darwish and Sheikh Imam, the venues were sold out. 'There is word going around that the audience want most of the low-standard commercial songs they hear today. But it turns out that the audience doesn't want that at all, they want someone to respect and listen to them. And if they're coming to hear the songs of Sayyed Darwish and Sheikh Imam, it means they want to hear these kinds of songs.'

I asked whether, aside from respect for the artistic message, Eskenderella are still singing these songs because of their social message. 'Yes, of course. But the point is, honest art changes people. Without having to give it any name such as jazz, political, social or emotional. Just perform honest art and you will not only change people, but you yourself will change.' Eskenderella are yet to release an album, but they do perform live in Cairo on a regular basis. **KA**

also honest, individual artists who are *abna' bi'athum*, children of their environments, who have chosen to express themselves, their perspectives, their experiences and their ideas with sincerity.

For me, the beauty of the Middle East as a whole lies in the shared yet individual local details that belong to each of its regions and sub-regions. This is how my love for the oud grew, for it is one of the few instruments that is capable of partaking in all of these traditions. From the folk songs of the Lebanese mountains to the Iraqi *maqam* (semi-improvised vocal), from the Egyptian port songs of Said to the *qudud* (poetic song form) of Aleppo. It is all different, but somehow interrelated. It may be impossible to highlight precisely the points where these traditions meet, but you can't deny a connection.

When I listen to the contemporary music of the region, I feel that I'm hearing a shared history in the making: real postcards of our times, honest documents of personal, social and cultural experience, be they positive or negative or anywhere in between. This is the magic of these artists' work and I hope for it all a long and prosperous future. ❐

© Khyam Allami
39(3): 82/95
DOI: 10.1177/0306422010381173
www.indexoncensorship.org

Khyam Allami performed at the Proms and Womad this summer. He is the first recipient of BBC Radio 3's World Routes Academy scholarship. www.khyamallami.com

DIVINE COMEDY

Portraits by
Chaza Charafeddine

BODY AND SOUL

Artist **Chaza Charafeddine** explains how popular notions of beauty were the inspiration for her series of portraits *Divine Comedy*

The *Divine Comedy* series is inspired by the Islamic art of the Mughal period and by Persian miniatures produced between the 16th and 18th centuries. I was also interested in images produced in the 1940s in the Middle East and the Indian sub-continent, depicting mythological beasts such as the *buraq* – part-human, part-horse – as well as animals that symbolise virtues, such as the peacock. My aim was to explore the aesthetics of popular representations of beauty, in particular the portrayal of female pop stars, whose perfection places them in an unearthly realm, closer to mythological creatures.

In the 1940s, popular art depicted the human part of the *buraq* as female, whereas in the past its gender had been ambiguous. From the Mughal dynasty until the late 18th century, there was an equal fascination with male beauty: in poetry of the period, there are frequent references to young, beardless men as the ideal form.

When I began the project, I initially wanted to work with young women who resembled well-known pop stars. I was also searching for the male looka-like of the Lebanese artist Bassem Feghali, who performs as a transvestite.

But the girls I photographed lacked that certain 'je ne sais quoi', that daring, if frivolous, sparkle in the eye; for frivolity in a pop star has a particular appeal. The only person to possess that allure almost effortlessly was Alex, the man I picked to represent Bassem. Alex's look and presence was actually even more intense.

So I decided to work with transsexuals, transgenders and transvestites as models, and base the pictures on the aesthetics of 16th and 17th century artists. Such an approach carries many possible interpretations and applications. To me, the most important aim was to shed light on the notion of ideal beauty, which, if it could ever exist, might perhaps only be embodied in a third sex combining male and female.

We would meet at my studio. My models talked to me about their daily lives, the difficulty of living as women in the bodies of men and of their psychological plight, but also of the problems they face in a society that cannot bear the existence of a gender it cannot place: is he a woman trapped in the body of a man? If so, why doesn't he just make things easier for us and accept being labelled as an effeminate man? And what's the difference between a transgender, a transsexual and a homosexual? Surely pretending to feel like a woman in a man's body must be the sign of a psychological disorder or an inflated narcissism?

Even in gay and lesbian circles, if not mocked, they are certainly marginalised, and their suffering is not taken seriously. The greatest dilemma remains that of the transgender, such as G, with whom I worked. Biologically a man, he says that he feels he is a woman, yet his sexual orientation is straight. Is G then a lesbian man? 'He is definitely making fun of us,' said a homosexual friend of mine, who believes that all men are deep down just like him. And as if the personal distress of having their bodies mismatched with their souls was not enough, they have to deal with their families' rejection and the difficulty, if not impossibility, of finding a job to sustain a living – adding to their tribulation, which is boundless.

We would speak of all this, and after a session or two we would begin the photo shoot. I would ask them about the image of the woman they dreamt of being, and I would try to transform them into that woman through make-up and clothes. Sometimes they would mention stars they wished to look like and sometimes, when they were unsure of who they wanted to be, I would suggest a star with whom I could see a resemblance. We have many pictures of Lebanese stars, but there are also stars nobody knows: the subjects of *Divine Comedy*, as themselves. ❐

Captions

Pages 97–98: L'ange Gardien II. *Background:* The Fly of the Simurgh, *circa 1590.* Signed Basawan. Prince Sadruddin Aga Khan Collection.

Page 99: Dame aux Fruits

Page 100: [LHS] Sans Titre VIII. *Original imprint of the horse: anonymous artist (end of 19th century). Printed in Pakistan around 1960. Background: Calligraphy by Alya Karame, Mughal ceramic*

[RHS] Sans Titre 1. *Original imprint of the horse, anonymous artist (end of 19th century). Printed in Delhi around 1960. Background: Ottoman embroidery*

[Bottom] Plate 1, Let's walk and talk. *Background: different plates from the gardens of paradise. Produced in the 15th century at the illumination workshop of Herât in Khurasan. From the* Illumination Manuscript

Page 101: Der Himmel über Beirut. *Original imprints of the horses: anonymous artists (end of 19th century, India, Egypt or Pakistan)*

Page 102: Sultane. *Background: Portrait of Sultan Abdul-Hamid II and Sultan Mahmud II from the Ottoman Empire.*

Page 103: L'ange Gardien I. *Background: 'The Angel of Tobias', circa 1590, signed Hosein*

Page 104: L'oiseau du Paradis II. *Original imprint of the peacock anonymous artist (end of 19th century). Background: details from different plates of the* Illumination Manuscript *depicting paradise. Produced in the 15th century at the illumination workshop of Herât in Khurasan*

Page 104: L'oiseau du Paradis I. *Background: original imprint of the peacock anonymous artist (end of 19th century). Background: Mughal ceramic*

©Chaza Charafeddine
39(3): 97/107
DOI: 10.1177/0306422010380511
www.indexoncensorship.org

Chaza Charafeddine lives and works in Beirut as a freelance artist and writer. *Divine Comedy* was exhibited at Green Art Gallery in Dubai earlier this year. A solo exhibition opens at the Agial Gallery in Beirut on 23 September and will run until October. www.agialart.com

WORDSANDMUSIC

Femi Kuti on
Beng Beng Beng

My song 'Beng Beng Beng' was a simple, light-hearted love song coming from an African man's perspective. I believe it was banned [in 1999] because there were other very political songs [on the album] that they didn't want the radio stations to play. So banning 'Beng Beng Beng' was like telling the journalists and radio stations, 'Don't touch this album.' It was very popular in general, and everybody knew about it, but the radio stations never gave it airplay. I don't think the lyrics were even offensive; it was less offensive than 'Let's Talk about Sex, Baby', but they played that for a long time on the radio stations. When they banned 'Beng Beng Beng' the stations were forced to stop playing anything sexual for a while.

I was becoming too popular, too political, everybody was listening to me. People who didn't even know about my father [Fela Kuti] were getting to know about me, then getting to know the whole story about my father. So I was getting to be a very big story.

My next album was angrier, more direct. The Shrine, my club in Lagos, was open and we played it live there, where it's always full – we always have about 2,000 people. And they always try to close the club. The last time they tried there was so much international talk about it that they opened it after a week and a half. Everyone was outraged – and not just in Nigeria. There is more pressure coming from outside than inside. Now the government is trying to be accepted by the international community, they are trying to pretend they're not corrupt, they pretend that everything is OK. Now, if somebody like me is shouting, 'No, that's wrong!' and they then ban my club, stop my music, then *they* are wrong, *they* are lying.

We don't have a lot of activists here in Nigeria. If you want airplay, you can't be an activist. So a lot of artists sing silly songs or love songs. But every artist, especially every young artist, either pledges their support silently or directly to The Shrine. So if The Shrine says, 'We want you to come and play,'

Beng Beng Beng
Femi Kuti

Beng beng beng beng beng
Beng beng beng beng
The time is 12, midnight my brother
The girl leave, out of my bed now
The weather outside na correct weather
That kind of cold freezing weather
Wey ego make your battery echarge extra
I say everything make correct order
The girl fine, I mean she so fine o
Her body, kai, na wahala
Anashiri just makes me wonder
Her breast be like e don love marry
I say everything make correct order
She said, love me, Femi don't stop
She said, squeeze me, now now
She said, love me, Femi don't stop
She said, squeeze me, now now
Beng beng beng, I just dey go o
Beng beng beng, I just dey go o
She said, love me now
She said, squeeze me now
To the left now, don't slow down now
To the right now, don't come too fast
To the left now, don't slow down now
To the right now, don't come too fast
She said, love me now
She said, squeeze me now
Beng beng beng, I just dey go o
Beng beng beng, I just dey go o
Lyrics published by kind permission of Femi Kuti

they will come and play their love songs, but they will play in solidarity. We have a festival, 50 of them will come and perform to show their support. But because they need to make a living, they will play love songs.

In my father's time, the media outside Nigeria were more silent, and nobody really knew how big my father was on the outside. Now, with so many radio stations you can pick up in Nigeria, with the internet, the Nigerian state can be exposed. People make phone calls now. In the 70s, it wasn't like that. Not everybody had a phone. Now, something happens, and anybody can pick up the phone, and say 'Hey! You know what? The police have closed Femi's club!' It was like wildfire. In my father's time, there was no network, so they could shut him in and oppress him. But then, I don't think my father knew how popular he was on the outside. He definitely didn't know how to capitalise on an international network. Being close to understanding the media, and everything that's going on, I can do it quickly. My father, he relied more on the Nigerian press to pass information. The Nigerian government could keep on attacking and silencing him, and it was like he was alone. Now, because of what he has been through, I think it's impossible to use that same tactic on me. The press belongs to the government, so they have tried saying I'm crazy in the press, that they've seen me walking the streets naked. They lie.

But they're losing the battle very fast. I was in South Africa, I was at the World Cup opening. The government had no way of knowing that I was going to be there until the very last minute. Nigerians appreciate it, they're like, 'Oh, that's our man! Yeah!' So it's very hard. They don't know how big I am, internationally, they don't know how I'm loved, so they have a problem. They are corrupt, they are thieves. I'm not saying it because I want to be popular. I'm saying it because they are making too many people miserable, and they are ruining too many lives in Africa. I'm very tactical in my approach, because I understand what's going on. They will try to silence me. I was attacked when I was going home [earlier this year]. They had about 15 people with clubs and knives and they were waiting for me just outside my house. I think that they were sent by the government, so I have more security around now.

I'm not as angry as ten, five years ago. Now I'm over it, on top of it. I think I was more angry because I was shocked. And so, I stopped smoking, I stopped doing anything that the government could use as an excuse for my protest songs. Now I'm more confrontational, I'm more direct. So they can't give the excuse, of 'Oh, he's on dope.' It's like playing chess, playing a game: they have no reason, no excuse to say anything negative about me.

They had a lot of negative things to say about my father: 'He has too many wives, he's smoking, he's this, he's that,' and that was a reason to always tell the people not to believe his songs.

The state is irrelevant to me now. I'm not afraid. They should not make me carry a gun. If they attack me again, I will carry a gun. I'm not afraid at all of speaking my mind and being there, but if I'm physically touched, like my father, I will change my mind. For now I have my microphone. My trumpet is my Uzi. ❏

Femi Kuti was talking to Lizzie Rusbridger
©Femi Kuti
39(3): 108/111
DOI: 10.1177/0306422010380512
www.indexoncensorship.org

CAN MUSIC KILL?

Louise Gray considers the troubling history of music and violence, from gangsta rap to Rwanda

Dubula, dubula (Shoot, shoot)
Aw dubul'ibhunu (Shoot the Boer)
Dubula, dubula (Shoot, shoot)
From 'Ayesaba Amagwala' (The Cowards are Scared)

Towards the end of March 2010, a case brought by a businessman in Delmas, a farming town about 40 miles east of Johannesburg, reached the regional high court in South Gauteng. Willem Harmse had applied for a ruling to stop another local businessman, Mohammed Vawda, from using the words '*Aw dubul'ibhunu* (Shoot the Boer)' on banners and singing them during a march, scheduled for 9 April, against the high crime rates in Mpumalanga and Gauteng. Vawda argued that the use of the Zulu lyrics, taken from the apartheid-era song 'Ayesaba Amagwala' (The Cowards Are Scared), was symbolic and, as such, referred to a repudiation of apartheid. Harmse, on the other hand, argued that the lyrics promoted hatred.

In the event, the court agreed with the plaintiff. On 26 March, Judge Leon Halgryn ruled that the use of the 'Shoot the Boer' song was unconstitutional and unlawful. (Literally, the Afrikaans word 'boer' means 'farmer', but it has been employed as a metaphoric term to signify South Africa's white Afrikaaner settlers since the 1880s.) South Africa's ruling African National Congress reacted quickly: 'The ANC is shocked and disappointed by the ruling of the South Gauteng high court that the ANC struggle song "Ayesaba Amagwala" is unconstitutional,' read its statement released the same day. Its national spokesman, Jackson Mthembu, said that the ANC would challenge the ruling at the constitutional court, adding, 'We believe that this song, like many others that were sung during the struggle days, is part of our history and our heritage. It will be very unfortunate if, through our courts, our history and our heritage were to be outlawed.'

This was not a court case based on semantics. There was a toxic background to the Boer song. Julius Malema, the president of the ANC's youth wing and a powerful populist figure with considerable personal ambition, had been singing 'Shoot the Boer' to whip up personal support in a constituency that, despite a decade of ANC rule, has seen little progress in its own hopes for economic prosperity.

Halgryn's ruling – a ban that extended to both speech and publication of the offending words – was supported a few days later at the high court in Pretoria. On 1 April, Judge Eberhard Bertelsmann said that democracy in South Africa was fragile and the ban against singing it was reiterated. Within hours, Malema arrived in Zimbabwe and joined Zanu-PF crowds singing

'Ayesaba Amagwala' and where – in contravention of the ANC's own policy – he commended President Robert Mugabe's land-grabbing policies.

All this struck raw nerves back home. Despite the considerable achievements of Nelson Mandela and the first black majority regime in South Africa, the country has formidable problems. Crime levels are high, and not simply for theft and the violent offences that fall short of killing. Since 1994 and the end of apartheid, more than 3,000 farmers – the majority of them white – have been murdered in the Rainbow Nation.

On 3 April, the former white supremacist leader Eugene Terreblanche joined their number, hacked to death by two young black farmworkers. So began for South Africa a crisis that was reported by a world media already primed for the start of the 2010 World Cup, a tournament that, it had been suggested, the country was incapable of hosting successfully. As the world's press churned out stories about South Africa's crime figures, about ANC corruption, about its catastrophic HIV/Aids rate, it seemed that the collapse of a much-vaunted racial harmony was on the agenda.

Few, if any, of the characters introduced thus far are, to use a phrase that none of them would like, whiter than white. Harmse's case was supported by Afriforum, the Afrikaaner civil rights group. Terreblanche was a failed demagogue with a violent past: he had served time for the attempted murder of a black man. Malema is a firebrand with a talent for inserting himself into the news. (For example, he played a part in fomenting South Africa's anger against the International Association of Athletics Federations when the Caster Semenya story broke in 2009.) And at the point when church leaders and moderate politicians in South Africa, including Helen Zille, leader of the opposition Democratic Alliance, were trying to defuse tension, Malema repeated his contempt of court on 8 April at a press conference, singing 'Shoot the Boer'.

So far, says Zille, the voice of moderation has prevailed. 'Julius Malema is a law unto himself,' she told the BBC on 9 April. 'He thinks he is above the law and above popular opinion. He knows he wants to build the base of his support on populism ... He infuriates people, but what infuriates people even more is that President Jacob Zuma does not draw a line in the sand and call him to account, tell him that he cannot sacrifice our future to his personal ambition ... [Zuma] needs to tell him we have a constitution in this country, and in a constitutional democracy institutions function; we have the rule of just law and due process and we don't have random individual rebel-rousers putting themselves above the law to mobilise for a revolution that they never experienced.' This was intended to hurt, and one suspects it did.

For Zille, lyrics such as 'Shoot the Boer' create a context 'in which murder is romanticised and legitimised'. It suggests, in the context of fragile democracy identified by the Pretorian judge, that extralegal action is justified. 'We don't want to be extremists,' Zille said. 'We realise that extremists could take us into a future we have done so much to avoid and that has really galvanised the moderate majority in South Africa.' She warned of the dangers of populism: extremes grow and the middle ground diminishes. 'Both Terreblanche and Malema erode that middle ground.'

The Malema case is significant because it raises, once more, the question of freedom of expression. Should everyone be able to say what they want? How would it have been, asked Harmse, outside the South Gauteng court, had he sung about killing a black man? (It was a rhetorical question: he had argued against the incitement of racial hatred.) Even if one did, on the grounds of a macabre quid pro quo, support anyone's freedom to do such a thing, it would surely be a theoretical position.

But the 'Boer Song', as it's since become known to non-Zulu speakers the world over, is also of interest because it raises an additional issue: the mode of its delivery. Music has, since time immemorial, played a major role in galvanising groups of people. Countries have anthems. Identifiable communities have their preferred songs, styles and modes of delivery. Sometimes the song does not conform to the community's self-image: when Serge Gainsbourg recorded his 'Aux Armes et caetera', his reggae rendition of France's national anthem 'La Marseillaise' in 1978, he received death threats from military veterans of the Algerian War and, on one occasion, hundreds of French paratroopers rioted at one of his concerts. When Jimi Hendrix coloured 'The Star-Spangled Banner' with screeds of guitar feedback at Woodstock in 1969, many establishment figures, embroiled at the time in the Vietnam War and committed to a stately version of a national anthem, were appalled.

Louise Gray's playlist

Cop Killer
Body Count
Warner Bros

Aux Armes et caetera
Serge Gainsbourg
Mercury

Boom Bye Bye
Buju Banton
Heartbeat Europe

Singing, especially, binds a community. It is a profound emotional activity. Soldiers sing; football fans sing; no Last Night of the Proms would be complete without lusty renditions of 'Rule Britannia' and 'Land of Hope and Glory'. Singing can be important for nation-building. The Nazis elevated one marching song, 'The Horst Wessel Song', to an anthem in 1930. Soon after the foundation of the State of Israel in 1948, community singsongs were organised across the country on a regular basis to foster a sense of esprit de corps as well as deliver a new language – Hebrew – to the country's multilingual population. (As one might expect, the dispossessed Palestinians developed their own songs of mourning.)

In general, none of this is problematic. No one expects promenaders to flood out of the doors of the Royal Albert Hall and start beating up foreigners on Kensington Gore, whatever the jingoistic messages of the evening's songs. These days, even football fans can usually be relied on to behave themselves. Even when music is used to profess a sentiment contrary to any dominant discourse – one thinks, perhaps, of gangsta raps such as NWA's 1988 'Fuck Tha Police' or Body Count's 1992 'Cop Killer', both songs that attracted radio bans and the displeasure of the authorities – there is usually a strong enough social mechanism that can absorb any perceived call to action. (In the case of gangsta rap, it's often because its consumers are not oppressed ghetto inhabitants but affluent, white teenagers.) In politically stable countries, examples of music being cited as an incitement to violence – as, for example, Marilyn Manson's bombastic, spectacular rock music in the case of the Columbine School killings of 1999 – are very rare. (And even here, it was later discovered that neither of the Columbine killers were fans of Manson's alienated goth rock.)

Similarly, there are occasions when one form of music is judged to be prejudicial to the right to a quiet life. In the case of 'murder music' (the phrase comes from gay activist Peter Tatchell to designate music that contains homophobic messages), reactions have been stringent – at least in the UK and US. Tours have been cancelled and many pressure groups are operational: Tatchell, at OutRage! in the UK, has long campaigned against homophobic music, while in Jamaica (*Time* magazine asked if it was 'the most homophobic place on earth') he has conducted brave work to draw attention to the worst manifestations of murder music. Buju Banton, whose 1992 hit, 'Boom Bye Bye', contained the choice lyric *'(Me say) Boom bye bye/ Inna batty bwoy (gay man's) head/ Rude bwoy no promote the nasty man/ Dem haffi dead'* was subjected to enormous commercial pressure to rescind the songs, although there is no clear evidence that he has done so. Beenie

Simon Bikindi before the International Criminal Tribunal for Rwanda, 2 December 2008
Credit: Ho New/Reuters

Man, whose 'Roll Deep' expresses similar sentiments – '*Roll deep mother-fucka, kill pussy-sucker (lesbian) /Roll deep motherfucker, kill pussy-sucker/ Tek a Bazooka and kill batty-fucker/Take a bazooka and kill bum-fuckers*' – was dropped from a high-profile MTV showcase in 2004 and had a UK tour cancelled. Both musicians are reported to have signed the Reggae Compassionate Act, a petition organised by OutRage!'s Stop Murder Music campaign, although, once again, the reports are unclear. (Beenie Man later explained: 'We don't need to kill dem [gays and lesbians]. We just need fi tell the people dem the right ting because I not supporting a gay lifestyle because it's not wholesome to me.'

The number of musicians who fall into the category of producing homo-phobic music is large. While Beenie Man, Buju Banton, Elephant Man and Jah Rules might appeal to a niche audience, it includes crossover stars such as Eminem, Ice Cube, DMX and Public Enemy. It's depressing that rap and reggae are reflected most audibly in this genre, even if murder music is not confined to these formats. Some major artists have broken rank, but none more eloquently than Kanye West, who urged his fans to 'break out of the mental prisons of [homophobia]'. Speaking from the stage of a 2008 concert, he said: 'Open your minds. Be accepting of different people and let people be who they are.'

West's stance is exceptional, even if there are some who would choose to diminish its efficacy by suggesting that it is a strategic one: that is, his crossover appeal has brought him to an audience that is less likely to hold homophobic views. But this said, such generalisations are hugely problematic. Not all black rap and reggae musicians and fans are homophobic: indeed, there is a burgeoning gay hip-hop ('homohop') scene with its own stars – Cazwell, Yo Majesty, Hanifah Wallida and Deadlee – and styles. Nevertheless, it is unfortunate that rap, and in particular reggae, emanates from a society – the Caribbean islands – that does little to protect its gay and lesbian citizens.

Can music kill? No, but it can move people to kill

And it's in this situation – where neither state nor social structures are strong enough to uphold order – that the power of music to move crowds is to be feared most. In many cases, it has been used to reinforce an ethnic identity. After the collapse of the former Yugoslavia into war in the 1990s, singers such as Ceca (wife to the Serbian militia leader, Arkan) came to the fore with a form of high-octane techno known as Balkan turbo-folk. Described by social theorist Alexei Monroe as 'a high-tempo collision of a traditional folk (including nationalist songs) and contemporary dance rhythms', turbo-folk was very much the Serbian soundtrack of the period. Its pounding rhythms were pure Euro-disco, its melodies a confluence of the many currents of Balkan music, and its lyrics were allegorical: did, for example, the 'beloved' invoked by Ceca mean her lover or her country? Was Mitar Miric's 'Ne može nam niko ništa' (No One Can Touch Us) a celebration of Serbian nationalism? Even now, the song can be heard on YouTube accompanied by photos of Serbian fighters.

Turbo-folk bolstered the confidence of its Serbian consumers – it was banal, but it was also something of a backdrop. It was not state sponsored, and once the Balkan conflicts ended, so did the genre. But in 1994, a far more chilling example occurred in Rwanda, a country where music was directly employed by a Hutu-led state in a 100-day genocide that saw at least 800,000 Tutsis and moderate Hutus murdered.

Once described as 'Rwanda's Michael Jackson', Simon Bikindi is a skilled musician and dancer. He performed before John Paul II, when the pope visited the country in 1990. In a place where patronage was important, Bikindi was a director of a folkloric ballet, a civil servant and a songwriter much in demand. He wrote, says Jean Baptiste Kayigamba, a former Reuters correspondent and genocide survivor, 'beautiful poetry'. Bikindi was, in short, a well-connected Hutu working out his art.

Unfortunately, among Bikindi's works were long, rambling songs with titles such as 'Nanga Abahutu' ('I Hate these Hutus'), Bebe Sebahinzi ('The Sons of Sebahinzi') and 'Wasezereye' ('We Have Said Goodbye to the Feudal Regime'). Beautiful poetry they may be, but they also presented a hugely skewed version of Rwanda's explosive tribal history. Existing in a context in which ethnic violence was not unusual (the 1994 genocide was just the most recent, violent and murderous), they were dangerous texts – and in the lead-up to the start of the 100 days and during the genocide itself, Bikindi's songs were everywhere: they were broadcast at roadblocks, on Radio Télévision Libre des Mille Collines (RTLM), a radio station that gave its listeners updates of where the 'inyenzi' (literally, cockroaches; figuratively, Tutsis) were hiding and broadcast lists of those designated for death.

In 2001, Bikindi was arrested in the Netherlands and handed over to the UN's International Criminal Tribunal for Rwanda (ICTR). The six-count indictment alleged that 'Simon Bikindi's musical compositions and live performances and recruitment, training and command of Interahamwe [the main Hutu militia] were elements of the plan to mobilise civilian militias to destroy, in whole or in part, the Tutsi'. In 2008, Bikindi was found guilty of 'direct and public incitement to commit genocide' and sentenced to 15 years in prison. An appeal against the sentence failed earlier this year. His music is now banned in Rwanda.

What issues does the Bikindi case raise? The ICTR recognised that Bikindi (even though he was a shareholder in RTLM) had little control over the broadcasting of his music, which had an 'amplifying effect' on the progress of the genocide; that the songs – for example 'Wasezereye' – predated the genocide; that the prosecution failed to make its allegation of murder against him stick. But it also recognised that Bikindi was capable of controlling his own actions, one of which involved travelling around an area of Rwanda 'as part of a convoy of Interahamwe, in a vehicle outfitted with a public address system broadcasting songs', including his own.

Violence, and especially the organised campaign that Rwanda experienced, arises from complex social and political circumstances. It is the most fragile societies, places where alternate discourses are not heard, where there is no capacity to defuse tension, that are most at risk. Can music kill? No, but it can move people to kill, and music can be manipulated.

In the wake of the death of Eugene Terreblanche and South Africa's inability to rein in Julius Malema, Helen Zille was asked if she thought that it was the singing of 'Shoot the Boer' that provoked the murderers. 'I don't think it will be possible to draw a direct link,' she replied, 'but nevertheless words that romanticise killing create a context in which people see that as a legitimate way of solving problems. And that context is very worrying.' ❐

©Louise Gray
39(3): 112/120
DOI: 10.1177/0306422010379686
www.indexoncensorship.org

Louise Gray writes for the *Wire* and *New Internationalist*. Her *No-Nonsense Guide to World Music* was published in 2009 by New Internationalist

VOICE TO THE VOICELESS

Cameroonian singer **Lapiro de Mbanga** gives an exclusive interview to Daniel Brown from prison on protest, politics and the art of satire

Since his return from self-imposed exile in Nigeria and Gabon in 1985, Cameroonian musician Lapiro de Mbanga has been a constant thorn in President Paul Biya's side. During the past two decades the singer has composed a long list of biting texts on the socio-economic realities in his beleaguered country. Unlike fellow artists, he uses the local pidgin, mixing English, French and Douala to articulate the daily injustices he witnesses. This language, so rich in imagery it is hard to translate, is called Mboko talk. Lapiro (an acronym abbreviating his name Lambo Pierre Roger and adding his place of birth, the town of Mbanga) has thus become the idol of the downtrodden and forgotten workers who people the slums and bus stations of Cameroon. His songs echo the struggle for democracy of the late 80s and 90s.

Lapiro's songs – 'No Make Erreur', 'Pas argent no love', 'Kop Nie', 'Mimba We', 'Na You' – often flirted with censorship and provoked the ire of officials. But it was the 2008 composition 'Constitution Constipée' which really brought Lapiro face to face with the country's repressive justice system. This protest song denounced the amendment of the constitutional clause, which limited presidential mandates to two non-renewable seven-year terms. The lyrics mix humour and anger in calling for Biya to step down, since the *pacho* (old man) is *daya* (tired) and has outlived his usefulness. 'Constitution Constipée' was banned from the television and radio networks. But it became something of a rallying cry for thousands of youths, students and workers who took to the streets in February 2008 as they refused the constitutional change and the steep rise in the cost of living. Lapiro was arrested in April and accused of inciting violence and arson. In September 2008 he was sentenced to three years in the New Bell prison near Douala. This could be extended by another 18 months if he continues to refuse to pay the fine of 546,000 FCFA (around 830€).

Since the sentence was passed, the Danish-based NGO Freemuse has been leading an international campaign for his release (see pages 34-40). The US-based lawyers' advocacy organisation Freedom Now is monitoring the case. In June 2010, it urged UN Secretary-General Ban Ki-moon to call for Lapiro's release at a meeting with President Paul Biya that month. By then, the Mondomix music site had launched a free-for-download album in support of the singer. Meanwhile, Lapiro and his family have managed to survive and fight the case, partly thanks to winning the prestigious Freedom to Create Imprisoned Artist prize and its award of $25,000 in November 2009. In April 2010, the Writers in Prison Committee of International PEN launched a campaign to further help the beleaguered artist.

The calls are becoming more urgent as the health of the 53-year-old has deteriorated, following a typhoid attack in December, along with respiratory problems and lumbago. Sanitary conditions are reportedly poor in cell number 18, which Lapiro shares with 50 other prisoners. Until recently, they included the director of the Douala weekly newspaper *La Détente Libre*, Lewis Medjo, also sentenced to three years in prison for articles he wrote about Biya. Medjo was released in June 2010, two years early.

In early July 2010, Index on Censorship contacted Lapiro de Mbanga on his cell phone. Over two days, the artist shared his thoughts and vision. He was at times shaky but, through the conversation, it became clear that his voice remains strong and defiant.

Daniel Brown: You were arrested on 9 April 2008, just two days before parliament adopted the new constitution that you attacked in your song 'Constitution Constipée'. How are you?

Lapiro de Mbanga: Not so good. There are 3,000 prisoners here and the sanitary conditions are very bad. I'm coming up to 53 years old, and the lumbago I've been carrying with me for a few years has worsened. There is no hygiene here and we must share our most intimate moments with the other cellmates. I should have been taken to hospital for a consultation but my status as a political prisoner has meant I have not been allowed to go once in these two years. I somehow survived the typhoid attack in December by taking the antibiotics my wife Louisette brought me. It's fortunate she comes every few days. It's a five-hour round trip from Mbanga, it's taking a toll on her, too.

Daniel Brown: Could you describe your daily life?

Lapiro de Mbanga: You could say prison has taught me to be lazy. I sometimes feel like I'm someone who has nothing more to give in life. I wake at 7 to 8 every morning and watch my TV. I keep informed about the outside world thanks to TV5 [France's international station] or Radio France International. I eat, chat with the others in the cell, play Ludo, scrabble, draughts. It's impossible to compose in such an atmosphere. I need calm, serenity. Here, I cannot concentrate and write the thoughtful songs people expect of me.

We have penal rations twice a day. At 1pm we are given boiled corn and at 5pm there's rice in some warm water. It's the same every day. It's way below minimum requirements. My wife brings me food every two days, I couldn't survive otherwise. I've seen people die of hunger. It happens every day in Cameroonian prisons.

Normally, I should have no contact with the outside world. Telephones are illegal here. I'm speaking to you because we have to scheme like common crooks. In prison there are all kinds of trafficking going on, including this one. You pay guards to turn a blind eye. You know, in Cameroon you can buy everything. This country has been world champion in terms of corruption. It's everywhere and filters down to here.

Daniel Brown: Are you not frightened of the consequences of being so frank?

Lapiro de Mbanga: It's all part of my struggle. If I was the scared type I would never have started singing in 1985. I'm not going to start getting scared after all these years. My struggle has always been to denounce inequalities and danger is part of that mission. The only thing that has changed for me since

1985 is I'm at the head of a family with six children. I can guarantee my own security, but not theirs. I'm scared for them. But I have no choice. If you start such a struggle, somebody must pay. Still, my family is unhappy with such risk taking. That's why I think if I don't go into exile after this prison term, I won't survive very long out there – they'll kill me. Because it's obvious people in charge don't want to be confronted with somebody who stops them from just getting on with things.

Daniel Brown: The managing editor of the *Cameroun Express*, Bibi Ngota, was found dead in his cell on 22 April. He was another critic of the Biya regime, arrested with two other journalists on fraud charges. Officials said the death was due to infections related to the Aids virus, a statement his family has denounced as pure invention. Your reaction?

Lapiro de Mbanga: You don't die of Aids nowadays. There are retroviral drugs to keep you alive. That's too frivolous a statement. He died because of the poor sanitary conditions here. They refused to have him go to hospital, like me. Yet Ngota was just doing his job. We're not far from an assassination for political reasons. When people in power are defending their own personal interests, they're ready to do anything to preserve them. All in the name of state security. I also feel in danger. Before going to jail, they tried to kill me twice. First, they sent some soldiers to my house on the night of 2–3 March [three days after rioting in Mbanga ended]. They were people working for Biya. They were able to carry it out. Then, two weeks later, a government official came over with four policemen to kill me. When the two attempts failed they threw me in prison. So, you see, I don't feel safe in this country. My life is under threat here, mine and those of my family.

Daniel Brown: What exactly happened leading up to your arrest?

Lapiro de Mbanga: The national strike started on 25 February 2008. I had been in Douala for a concert on the 23rd and returned to Mbanga at 7.30pm on the 24th. I had decided to go back because these strikes are always concentrated in the cities. They never spread to towns with only 45,000 inhabitants like Mbanga. But on the 25th, I found the town had ground to a halt. This kind of thing hadn't happened since the big campaigns of 1991 and 92. This time, there were even demonstrations in front of the presidential palace in Yaounde. People were striking to protest the constitutional change and the hike in prices. In Mbanga, it was

the moto-taxis that were demonstrating against the rise in petrol prices. They had set up barricades in front of the home of the local police chief. I went to try to sort it out because I'm also a traditional chief in Mbanga. I'm responsible for good relations in District 12 where I live [there are 16 districts in Mbanga].

You know, I'm a leader of opinion here, I write about the society I live in. So I *had* to go. On the way, I found out there were high-school students who wanted to burn down their school. People also wanted to burn down the town hall. I stopped them all. I told them they would lose all their papers, their birth certificates and ID cards. On my way home, I went by people wanting to burn down the Total petrol station. 'Where are you going to buy your petrol afterwards?' I asked them. They listened to me and spared the station.

The next day, I heard people were attacking various big companies in Mbanga. There were the banana growers, the mineral water company and the company called SPM, the Société des Plantations de Mbanga. The SPM is half-owned by the French. I tried to stop the pillagers there but it was too late. What can you do when you are faced with 30,000 angry youths? I filmed it all with my camera, hoping the images would help in the inquest after. People were taking computers, documents, even stuff that was no use to them. Then, I returned home as the army moved in and the fighting got worse the next day.

I was safe, however. No one can attack me at home. Everyone knows I'm a defender of the common man (*le petit peuple*). The strike wasn't involving me directly. I'm the one who gives voice to the voiceless. Afterwards, however, the authorities accused me of calling on the people to go on the rampage. They were after me. The SPM said I was responsible.

Daniel Brown: But you and your defenders have always said it was your song 'Constitution Constipée' that is the real reason behind the arrest. What do you think the authorities feel is so dangerous about the lyrics you've written about the president?

Lapiro de Mbanga: The song denounces with humour the corruption and injustices in Cameroon. I just show what a masquerade the revision of the constitution is. And I attack Paul Biya without ever mentioning his name. I say: 'The father is tired, leave him alone.' I add: 'White collar bandits want to ransack the constitution of my country.' I say that presidential mandates are limited in the US and France, but not in Cameroon.

I sing that Cameroon is the 'birthplace of advanced democracy, it is peaceful, full of electoral frauds and a paradise for corruption. *We don't care*', I insist.

Daniel Brown: This use of humour and irony is characteristic of your work.

Lapiro de Mbanga: Yes, the most serious things in humanity must be said with a laugh and not with bitterness. I say serious things with lightness. It has always worked. When you laugh, things stick in your mind. And lots of Cameroonians listen to me. Eighty-five per cent of our population are marginalised. I'm their idol, their voice. I'm the one who takes the microphone into public places when they are demonstrating.

Daniel Brown: This is not the first time you have composed a subversive song. There was 'No make erreur' in 1986, talking about those living on the margins of society.

Lapiro de Mbanga: Yes. I was born in a small town. You have to see Mbanga to understand what misery is about here. We offer very cheap labour to anyone who wants it. That's why the Europeans have invested in the palm and banana industries here. People earn 20€ a month for 30 days of work on the banana plantations. They start at 5am and finish at midnight. All for 20€! People are suffering. How can they send their children to school on that salary?

Daniel Brown: 'No make erreur' has an *mboko* as the central character. These are conmen, swindlers, thieves plying their trade in public areas.

Lapiro de Mbanga: Yes, I have a certain vision of society. How do we create these *mbokos*? Where do they come from? Well, when their parents earn 20€ a month, they have no money to buy their kids a ball, a doll, or take them on a holiday. And they see the tiny privileged minority getting a bicycle and enjoying luxury. So, for them, it's steal or die. Here, in our prison, I see a lot of these children. The system pushed them to be thieves, they even end up robbing their own parents.

Daniel Brown: In 'Kop Nie', your 1988 release, you describe the common man whom you call the 'sauveteurs'. These men and women survive through petty trading of food or trinkets.

Lapiro de Mbanga: Yes, they also play hide and seek with the police. Yet, the state forces them to pay taxes. They are lumped with all the duties and none of the rights. They pay their taxes and get nothing in return. Informal when they work, formal when they're fleeced (*laughs*).

Daniel Brown: In this song, we see how important public spaces are for you: the bus or train stations, the markets.

Lapiro de Mbanga: Ha, Cameroon has a Ministry of Transport. But there is no public transport, no buses, trains or planes. We're the only state in the world with a transport ministry which has no policy for public transport. It's a nation where the people have to privatise and improvise. For example, you must buy the worn-out European cars to get around. That's why we have a record rate of road accidents here. There are a huge number of deaths as a result (*pause*). When I talk about all of this I become very bitter. But I have no choice. It's the truth.

Daniel Brown: Moving on to your next hit, 'Mimba We'. Here, you engage the government with the people's grievances. You appeal directly to the president for him to intervene.

Lapiro de Mbanga: The government must do something *for* its people, not against its population. It's supposed to be there to serve the people. That's why the English call it 'civil *servants*' [in English]. The state is not supposed to wage a war against the people it cannot house, educate, or keep healthy. No wonder they can't feed themselves. I call it a genocide against the people. There is no other word for it.

Daniel Brown: In the early 90s, there was an effervescent call for popular participation in politics in this country. At the time you released 'Na You', which accuses Biya of messing up the country. You called on him again to clean things up.

Lapiro de Mbanga: This is about a president who has no links with his people. Cameroon is divided in regions with powerful local leaders. Yet Biya spends *no* time with them, he hasn't in the 30 years he's been in power. He lives in Switzerland more than here. But he listens to my songs, otherwise I wouldn't be in this prison. He has developed a very sophisticated secret service, it's a legacy from his predecessor [Ahmadou Ahidjo, whom Biya succeeded in November 1982]. Even this exchange with you is being taped by them. How do I know? I know. Cameroon is a police state.

Daniel Brown: Apart from Freemuse, there have been a number of initiatives abroad to have you released. One such effort was a letter written to Carla Bruni-Sarkozy, also a musician, in an attempt to rally her to your cause. Yet, her husband [President Sarkozy] has been greeting Paul Biya with open arms ever since he took office in 2007. What do you think of France's position over your incarceration?

Lapiro de Mbanga: Yes, a committee called the Collectif des Organisations Démocratiques de la Diaspora Camerounaise, or CODE, wrote to Carla Bruni. But she has done nothing till this day. So, Nicolas Sarkozy and Paul Biya are part of the same system. You must understand one thing, however: I'm not asking to be freed. I just want a real, equitable trial. Out of the 3,000 prisoners here, 2,600 have not been judged. They stay years like this. So, in Cameroon there is not a presumption of innocence, but one of guilt.

I don't believe in this justice system. It cannot be independent when the man at its helm is the president who put me in prison. I appreciate people calling on me being freed. But I want no pardon. I want an international penal court to try me, with three international magistrates. If I'm guilty, then let them sentence me to 50 years in jail.

I filed a complaint against the magistrate who condemned me because I believe he changed someone's testimony, what we call in French *faux dans l'acte*. I sent the complaint to the Supreme Court and they have remained silent ever since. That was three months ago.

I want no pardon. I refuse it. A pardon is for a guilty party and I'm not guilty. I want justice without a pardon. I want to be freed in the normal way. It's the same thing concerning the fine of 546,000 FCFA. If I pay it, it would be like admitting I was guilty. Too bad if I have to stay another 18 months behind bars.

Daniel Brown: But if you were released in April 2011, you could be involved in the next general elections.

Lapiro de Mbanga: You must understand: I am no opponent to Biya! Because if you change Biya tomorrow, nothing will change. He's just part of a system that is directed by the Quai d'Orsay [Ministry of Foreign Affairs] in Paris. I'm

no idiot. I'm not naive. If the successor of Biya does not want to die, he has to be the same as Ahidjo and Biya. People have to stop saying we're celebrating 50 years of independence this year. Cameroon is not independent! ❑
Daniel Brown's interview with Lapiro de Mbanga was conducted in French

© Daniel Brown
39(3): 121/130
DOI: 10.1177/0306422010381329
www.indexoncensorship.org

Daniel Brown is a senior staff reporter in the English service of Radio France International. He is also vice-chair of Freemuse and a regular contributor to *Songlines*

COFFEE-HOUSE BLUES

Turkish novelist **Kaya Genç** talks to Kurdish musicians about making their voices heard despite continuing discrimination and prejudice

I have been sitting in this coffee house for a while now, drinking a large cup of Americano and listening to *Rewend* ('Nomad', a Kurdish song) through my earphones for the third time. It is a curious song: I don't have a clue what it is about and yet the vocal is profoundly moving and strangely familiar. 'The night is dark, it is pitch black/I have lost my senses; the darkness has made me mad.' It seems to come from the mountains high above the Anatolian plateau, from heights only eagles can reach. 'Like a parched thistle swept up by the wind/I am without place and time.' The voice travels across the country and, as I suddenly realise, my being. It has no centre, it is a voice that belongs to all places and all times. 'Like the prey of a merciless eagle/I was swept high and mercilessly plunged deep.'

The performer of the song, Aynur, appears in Fatih Akın's beautifully vibrant 2005 documentary *Crossing the Bridge: The Sound of Istanbul*, where she sings in the delicate acoustics of a hamam, a Turkish bath. I went to meet her at the headquarters of Sony Music in Istanbul.

'When the audience perceives me as a creative soul, it is a wonderful feeling,' she tells me during our interview in a depressing conference room.

'But there are times when you don't have a clue what the reaction may be. I try to figure out the reaction and at that precise moment I am no longer free. But we all know that music is about the freedom of the soul, and in moments of anticipation that is taken from me.'

Aynur isn't sure who her audience is. Is it mainly Kurds, or does she have more Turkish fans? She cannot be certain. But she knows that among her listeners are angry souls, those who seek to ban her music along with all other Kurdish music. In an article published in December 2007 in the ultra-nationalist *Türksolu* ('the Turkish left'), a columnist complained of the so-called 'Kurdisation' of Turkey's culture: 'When I turn on the television it is filled with Kurdish serials and films,' the columnist protested. 'And when I seek solace in music, all I have is Kurdish songs, Kurdish music videos. Getting onto a minibus I realise that they are playing a Kurdish song! "Is it Kurdistan?" I ask myself. On the way home I meet drug-dealers, pimps, gays and transvestites. It is a strange coincidence that they are all Kurds!'

While such articles that appear to incite hatred are freely distributed in the country, Kurdish musicians such as Aynur still suffer from the discriminatory laws of the Turkish Republic. Her album *Keçe Kurdan* ('Kurdish Girl'), released in 2004, was banned by a court in Diyarbakir, in south-eastern Turkey, in 2005, although the ban was lifted later that year. The problem was with the title song, composed by Şivan Perwer, perhaps the most influential Kurdish musician alive – he fled to Germany in 1976 and now lives in exile in Germany. 'It was a song against the oppression of women,' Aynur explains. 'But they took it to be a call to arms.'

There are signs, however, of a more liberal atmosphere in the country. A year after Aynur's album was banned, she made a guest appearance in *Gönül Yarası* (Lovelorn), an extremely popular film seen by almost a million viewers in Turkey. Her latest album, *Rewend*, has been an instant hit. A prominent figure at European festivals, Aynur's admirers include Martin Scorsese, Keith Richards, Emir Kusturica and Robert De Niro. Recently, Johnny Depp visited her backstage and asked whether he could play alongside her group. 'Why not?' she answered.

Publications ranging from the London *Times* to the *New York Times Magazine* have used her image on their front pages as a representative of a blooming cultural ethos in Turkey. She is proud of her position but shows no signs of arrogance. 'I am singing in sold-out concerts all over the world. But sadly there are still prejudices in my homeland,' she says. 'Of course, a great deal has changed over the past decade. Organisers would unplug my jack ten years ago.' In 2010, Aynur began working with Sony Music in Turkey,

Aynur in the documentary Crossing the Bridge: The Sound of Istanbul, *2005*
Credit: Everett Collection/Rex Features

which created a sub-label that will release its first albums this autumn, totally devoted to Kurdish music – in Turkey and Iraqi Kurdistan.

It was Ayhan Evci, a Kurdish producer and composer living in Hamburg, who came up with the idea of the new label and put the idea to Sony. He has collaborated with musicians such as Ciwan Haco, a popular figure in Kurdish music, as well as many alternative Turkish and German artists. 'We could no longer work with the traditional recording companies in Turkey,' he says. 'Kurdish music grew less productive for a while and the sales were low. We needed new means of production, international standards.' The new label is called Pel ('Leaf' in Kurdish). 'It is a small but important step for Kurdish music. If we manage to produce first-class records then perhaps luck will be on our side as well.'

How things change. Only a decade ago it was a far-fetched fantasy for anyone to imagine Kurdish being performed on stage, let alone distributed via international labels. As the success of Aynur lightens my day, I take a look at the newspaper on the table, lying next to the half-filled cup. 'A new court case for Kurdish singer Ferhat Tunç, who will be tried in accordance with certain comments he has made during a concert,' the liberal daily *Radikal* reports. 'He risks up to 15 years in prison.'

I can no longer feel the warm summer sun above the tall buildings. The illumination is gone – replaced by the long shadows of skyscrapers. And no one seems to care. My memories take me back just over a decade ago to February 1999 when, on a cold winter's night in Istanbul, Ahmet Kaya, then the most popular Kurdish singer in the country, was invited to receive an award from the Association of Magazine Journalists and in the process suffered the worst case of character assassination in recent Turkish history.

It was a night to remember: cameras everywhere, filming the famous guests. Best-selling musicians were there, as well as newcomers, media moguls, journalists, television managers, models and Turkish playboys. Amidst the thick layer of cigarette smoke, Kaya was called to the stage. 'I take this award not only for myself but also for the Human Rights Association, Saturday Mothers [composed of mothers whose children had been 'lost' by the security forces] as well as journalists,' he said. Then suddenly he added: 'By the way, folks, in my next record I will have a Kurdish song for you. You know, I am Kurdish and I will be making a Kurdish video for this song. I know that there are courageous people here among us who will broadcast my video. I also know that they will have a hard time explaining to the Turkish people why they did not broadcast my video.'

This little speech sent shock waves through the media elite gathered in the ballroom of the hotel. 'Bastard!' one singer shouted. 'Go to hell!' another screamed. 'This is an insult to us, to the media! We shall respond!' a journalist complained. In moments, people had got to their feet; many musicians threw forks and spoons at Kaya, while Serdar Ortaç, a famous pop musician whose albums top the charts, began improvising a song on stage about Atatürk, the Turkish republic's modernist and modernising founder. He looked at Kaya and said: 'This country belongs to us, not to you strangers.'

There was total chaos. Kaya's wife, Gülden, feared her husband would be lynched in front of the cameras. But he managed to escape. That same week, the right-wing *Hürriyet* newspaper ran the headline 'An inglorious man!' with a photograph that attempted to link Kaya to the PKK (the Kurdistan Workers' Party), the terrorist organisation that has been fighting the security forces for more than three decades. Four months later, Ahmet Kaya, no longer feeling safe in his homeland, took a little bag, his *saz* (a traditional stringed musical instrument he excelled in playing) and caught a plane from Istanbul to Paris. He never came back. He died in November 2000 from a heart attack, barely two years after that night in Istanbul. He was 43.

With the memories of that notorious evening in mind, I visited the musician Ferhat Tunç (an old friend of Kaya's) in his office at Beyoglu, the crowded heart of Istanbul. He is currently facing prosecution. Because of anonymous death threats he has installed a special security system in the building – very similar to the one I have seen in Nobel laureate Orhan Pamuk's office.

'I simply attended a music festival,' Tunç says in his defence. 'The concert was not organised by the PKK. It was a legal event entitled "Culture, nature and peace festival". As a popular singer in the region, I regularly make speeches on stage about the recent events.' He had simply expressed the significance of a music festival organised in Eruh, the village where the terrorist PKK organisation conducted its first violent attack against the Turkish state in 1984. Since then, more than 30,000 people have died in the conflict between the PKK and the security forces. In July 1987, the Turkish state imposed martial law in Elazığ, Hakkari, Mardin, Tunceli, Van and Siirt (where Eruh village is located), during which period human rights violations committed by the security forces peaked. Martial law was lifted only in November 2002. Tunç told the audience that he was a witness to the atrocities committed during this time by the 'killers in uniforms' and that it was nice to know that while they were having a good time enjoying music that day 'those killers' were being tried in courts (in connection with the high-profile Ergenekon case, a number of military personnel, including former generals, had been arrested; they are being tried for crimes against the state.)

'And for these comments, I am accused of expressing the views of the PKK. Some newspapers swiftly labelled me as a member of the PKK. I feel less secure and more worried. I have never felt this worried in my life.' These words from a musician whose career spans 28 years. If convicted, he faces up to 15 years in prison.

Earlier this year, Tunç was awarded the Freedom of Expression Award by Freemuse, in association with Index on Censorship. 'For almost three decades, Ferhat Tunç has insisted on exercising his right to perform his music in spite of several court cases and other threats against him,' the award committee said in its nomination. 'He has continued to sing songs in the minority language Zaza (Dimli) and in Kurmanci (Kurdish) as well as Turkish. He has refused in a firm way to succumb to all the intimidations, but without expressing any hatred against his perpetrators. Ferhat has actively propagated the strengthening of human rights and democracy in Turkey.'

Tunç was born in Dersim (later Turkifed as 'Tunceli') in 1964, in the middle of a painful century for Turkish Kurds. 'Mine is a wounded history,' he says. 'And since my childhood, elegy was the dominant form in Kurdish culture. As a teenager I sang many Kurdish elegies. As I attended primary school, my connection with the Kurdish language was cut off. We were instructed to speak Turkish even in our households.' After secondary school, Tunç became interested in Marxist revolutionary songs; he felt that 'singing revolutionary songs was an important part of the process of revolution'.

As street fights between revolutionary youth and the US-backed nationalist groups reached new heights at the end of the 1970s, Turkish musicians found themselves facing difficult choices. 'Kurdish music was inevitably politicised,' producer Ayhan Evci explains. 'Kurdish language and culture were banned and Kurdish identity was rejected. Kurdish musicians responded to the growing militarisation with songs of resistance.' Then came the 1980 military coup that resulted in even more oppression for the Kurdish population. 'Musicians had to flee Turkey for European countries,' Evci remembers. 'And the atmosphere in Europe was even more political. These musicians felt a duty to compose political songs. The main source for the lyrics was the famous Kurdish poet Cigerxwin. Elegy was the dominant form but it had some experimental touches by the composers, which was interesting. In the immediate aftermath of the military coup, Şivan Perwer and Ciwan Haco were the big Kurdish musicians – Perwer representing the traditionalist approach while Haco combined European musical scores with old Kurdish songs.'

Kaya Genç's playlist

Delale
Aynur
Sony

Mahur
Ahmet Kaya
Raks

Sevmek Bir Eylemdir
Ferhat Tunç
Ideal Müzik

Like many of his contemporaries, Tunç left Turkey in 1979 and began a new life in Germany. He met American musicians and played his *saz* in a reggae band. Recording political songs in a little studio in Bremen, Tunç decided to return to his homeland in 1985. In 28 years he has recorded 21 albums whose titles express his struggle against oppression in different ways: *Yaşamak Direnmektir* ('Living is Resisting', 1988), *Kanı Susturun* ('Silence the

136

Ferhat Tunç at the Index on Censorship Freedom of Expression Awards, London, March 2010
Credit: Karim Merie

Blood', 1995), *Sevmek Bir Eylemdir* ('Loving is Action', 2005) and his latest, *Çığlıklar Ülkesi* ('Country of Cries', 2009). His albums regularly sell more than 750,000 copies, but like many musicians he depends largely on concerts. 'In the last five years it's been harder for me to have concerts in the western regions of Turkey,' he complains. 'I recently planned to have a large open-air concert in Manisa, but then I received an official letter announcing that the police will not be able to conduct the order and security of my concert ... So they had it cancelled and asked me to have my concert in a little wedding hall in the middle of summer. Concert organisers in Istanbul do not invite me as they are also afraid that there might be trouble during my performance.'

Discrimination against Kurdish musicians such as Tunç is not a new phenomenon. As Evci described to me from his flat in Hamburg, the Turkish state singled out Kurds and their culture during the 90s, when the conflict between the PKK and the security forces was at its height.

'To give a concert in Kurdish you needed special permission. Before having a concert, every Kurdish musician needed to go to the district attorney and return with documents declaring any criminal records. Turkish musicians did not undergo the same treatment. Distribution of Kurdish albums in Kurdish regions was prohibited.' According to Evci, the noughties brought new problems for Kurdish musicians as they now suffered from a system that did not let them get royalties for their albums. When the Turkish state opened a new state channel in Kurdish in 2009, TRT 6, the royalties problem still remained. 'German radio pays royalties for just one song, whereas TRT paid me nothing for all those Kurdish songs that I have composed.' This is perhaps the last nail in the coffin for Kurdish music: after political oppression comes financial depression.

Tunç, who also complains of the financial problems of Kurdish music, is the Turkish representative of the Denmark-based musical freedom organisation Freemuse. He was invited to Duke University, in the United States, last year to give seminars to graduate students in the music department. For two weeks he was treated for what he was, an authentic voice of ethnic music. When he came back to Istanbul, the political atmosphere was different. The Turkish prime minister, Recep Tayyip Erdoğan, conducted several breakfast meetings where he invited Turkish musicians, the literati and various groups of artists in order to discuss his vision of the democratisation of the Kurdish problem. Tunç was not invited to the session with the musicians; in fact, he thinks the government's rapprochement is rather 'fake' and 'not genuine'.

In April 2008, the Turkish government amended the contents of the notorious Article 301 of the penal code by replacing the expression 'insulting Turkishness' with 'insulting the Turkish nation' and making the justice secretary's approval mandatory before launching a prosecution. It also introduced new legislation relating to counter-terrorist activities, formulated in such a way that the likes of Tunç can be tried for aiding terrorist groups or propagating terrorist activities.

My colleague İrfan Aktan, a reporter at large for *Newsweek*'s Turkish edition was sentenced to 15 months in prison earlier this year for using a quote from a PKK member which, under the new legislation, is considered to be spreading terrorist propaganda. With the new anti-terror law, the range of crimes that may be considered as terrorist offences has increased dramatically. Crimes as different as sexual harassment, anti-military propaganda and prostitution may now be categorised as terrorist offences. 'Things need to change. The Turkish establishment nowadays questions its role in the Ahmet Kaya affair, but it is too late. Only the shrill voices of the ultra-nationalists could be discerned during that notorious evening. It is still the same. No one broadcasts Kurdish music videos and the establishment Kaya challenged is firmly in place.'

I had left Tunç's office with this grim conclusion on freedom of expression in Turkey. A few days later I called Naim Dilmener, a prominent music critic who has published many books and is a columnist for the daily *Radikal*. He is an energetic figure and nowadays his main obsession is Twitter, where he tweets endlessly on the frequent hate-filled articles in the Turkish media. 'When we talk about Kurdish music, we are also talking about the Kurdish language,' he says. 'They are both in chains. Now they can move more freely but the chains still remain.' In the years following the military coup, Kurdish music had inevitably veered towards propaganda. 'This is bad for any kind of music in any language,' Dilmener argues. 'Kurdish music needs songs about love and daily issues and common things as well. They need to embrace rock and rap vibes and new sounds. Kurdish musicians such as Çar Newa, Ciwan Haco, Mehmet Atlı, Rojin, Nilüfer Akbal and Ayhan Evci struggle for this kind of a renewal. They have not succeeded yet. But eventually, they will.'

I have been sitting in this coffee house for a while now, drinking another cup of Americano and listening to 'Delale' (My Beauty) for the first time. This song about rural life on a distant mountain is almost a transcendental experience. 'A wound remains with me,' the speaker in the song informs her lover, 'don't leave me my beauty. This world is like a blink of an eye/All that remains is pain and death.' As I pack my things to leave, 'This world is a dark and cruel place,' Aynur sings in her deep voice. 'Stay my beauty.' I feel a familiar urge to protect the lover, the beautiful voice that seems to come from high above the Anatolian plateau from the cruel country that I inhabit. But evidently it is too late. Too much has been lost and the voice within us is, and perhaps shall continue to be, a wounded one. ❐

©Kaya Genç
39(3): 131/139
DOI: 10.1177/0306422010379685
www.indexoncensorship.org

Kaya Genç's first novel, *L'Avventura*, was published in 2009. He is a PhD candidate at the English literature department of Istanbul University and is a reporter at large for *Newsweek*

ROCKING RANGOON

Hard rock and hip hop have been powerful vehicles for political dissent in Burma, writes artist and former political prisoner **Htein Lin**

Music, like all other art forms in Burma, has been subject to censorship since the advent of Ne Win's military regime in 1962. The censor then, as now, was as much concerned with silencing lyrics deemed culturally 'inappropriate' as blocking political content. Lyrics still have to be submitted for approval, and once this is obtained words and music are recorded and then resubmitted before a record can go on sale. Where politics is not an issue, the speed of getting approval is a matter of fame and kickbacks.

During the 70s and 80s, Burmese youth vented their frustration with living under a collapsing socialist regime through hard rock and heavy metal, with bands such as Iron Cross and singers Lay Phyu and A-ngeh. A few singers and lyricists attempted to write music touching on politics. The most famous Shan ethnic minority singer, Saing Htee Saing, broke into the Burmese mainstream, but also worked with lyricist Dr Sai Kham Leik to sing Shan language songs about independence, federalism and civil war. Songs about student life crept past the censors, carefully disguising allusions to the banned student union or the state of education. 'Khit lu-ngeh a-kyeh-kyat' – 'Today's youth are well-grounded' – criticised the state of education and its rewards, noting that while school dropouts have cars, university graduates only have a photo for their parents, and 'a pilot's licence but no chance to take off'. This song became particularly popular after the 1988 democracy demonstrations, when the universities were closed for years and professors sacked. Another anthem for the 1988 protests was Mun Awng's '8/82 Inya', named after a famous Rangoon campus student hostel.

Mun Awng was one of many musicians to participate in the 1988 demonstrations. He fled into exile in the student camps on the Thai border, where he wrote new songs including 'Eh-Soe' (Evil Visitor), a reference to the midnight knock on the door by military intelligence, and 'Tempest of Blood'. His music bled back inside the country to the reopened campuses. I also had to flee to the border in 1988 or risk arrest for leading the pro-democracy strike. When I returned from the jungles on the Indian, and later Chinese, borders and resumed my degree in 1993, a lot of students were listening to underground Mun Awng cassettes in their hostel rooms, just as we had in the camps.

Another up-and-coming singer who fled briefly to Three Pagodas Pass on the Thai border was Htoo Ein Thin. He returned to Rangoon, and his original song 'Yar Za Win Myar Ye Tha Doe Tha Mee' (History's Bride), although nominally about the river Irrawaddy, became popular as a resistance song alluding to Daw Aung San Suu Kyi.

Meanwhile, the military regime sought to use rock music for propaganda, with songs that criticised the exiled media and the opposition movements. It spotted talented composers in the ranks, such as Major Mya Than San, and forced famous musicians to sing their songs. Since many musicians had drug problems, they were easy to blackmail if they couldn't be bought, although some still resisted.

One famous singer who didn't resist was Zaw Win Htut and his band Emperor. His 1995 album, *Maha*, adopted a strong nationalist pro-military theme for which he is still resented today. It was this album which sparked a rerun of the teashop brawl over a cassette tape that ignited the student movement in 1988. *Maha* was being played in a Rangoon University campus teashop when a group of students, some of them my 1988 generation and former political prisoners, snatched the cassette and destroyed the teashop, threatening to do the same to any teashop that played it. Although the university rectors launched an investigation, the student leaders prevailed on them to drop it, and the faculty was anyway disinclined to pursue it in case it rebounded on academics' careers.

The incident was significant in that it served to mobilise a new generation of students who had not experienced 1988. Older activists who had returned to campus were able to talent-spot freshmen who showed an interest. The organising which followed led to the next round of student demonstrations in 1996.

The soundtrack for that period included two notorious political albums. In 1996, Lay Phyu and Iron Cross brought out *Power 54*, which included songs by Nyi Thit, now in exile. Aung San Suu Kyi was giving talks every weekend at her house, 54 University Avenue. The government spotted the significance of the album's title and all songsheets and cassettes were ordered to be destroyed. Iron Cross was eventually allowed to reissue the album, but under the name *Power*.

Ko Win Maw, of the band Shwe Thansin (Golden Melody), was not so lucky. In 1996 he was arrested and imprisoned for composing 'Spirit of the Fighting Peacocks' in support of Aung San Suu Kyi and her National League for Democracy (NLD). A few years later I found myself in Mandalay jail after a couple of '88 generation comrades wrote to one another that I might be up for resuming activism. Their letter was intercepted, and I experienced the midnight knock on the door that Mun Awng had sung about.

While I was in Mandalay jail, several of Win Maw's cellmates were transferred there from Toungoo jail, after a falling out between communist and non-communist political prisoners. From them I heard how my friend Win Maw had created a handmade guitar out of a plastic bowl, fishing line and a piece of wood. The prison guards appreciated his efforts, so he was allowed to make some more and teach other prisoners to play, forming a band that performed at political ceremonies. The story inspired me to paint his amazing improvisation as part of my series of paintings using old prison uniforms as canvas.

After his release in 2002, Win Maw had difficulties getting permission to perform. His musician brother, Win Zaw, had gone to Thailand and joined the Democratic Voice of Burma (DVB). He encouraged Win Maw to turn to video journalism and smuggle footage out to DVB-TV. Win Maw told me how he would hang around filming outside the NLD HQ in 2005 and 2006 dressed like a typical Special Branch officer. Special Branch assumed he was one of them, or from a rival government intelligence agency. But Win Maw was arrested again in November 2007 and sentenced to six years a year later for his role in sending footage of the Saffron Revolution out to the world. He is the veteran musician and mentor who features in the 2008 film *Burma VJ*. I am sure he is still playing inside Insein jail, although he was tortured badly following his arrest.

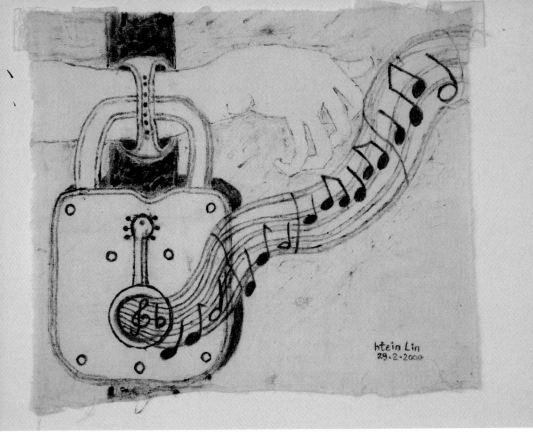

Prison painting of Win Maw's guitar
Credit: Htein Lin

When I was imprisoned in 1998, rock was still the dominant genre. I would have missed the rise of rap and hip hop had I not had access to a smuggled radio during the later period of my seven-year sentence. As a perceived western import, Burmese rap songs were not played on government radio, but I heard them on the BBC Burmese Service.

The godfather of Burmese rap is generally considered to be former sound engineer and sampler Myo Kyawt Myaing. But the so-called 'first generation' of Burmese rappers began with a group called ACID, who started out in Rangoon's burgeoning nightclub scene in the late 1990s. Its four members were Hein Zaw (who died in 2006), Anegga (son of famous rocker Min Min Latt, who used to sing Presley and Beatles covers), Yan Yan Chan and Zeyar Thaw. Their first album, *Sa-Tin-Chein* (Beginning), was an immediate hit in 2000, and is still seen as a seminal album in the history of Burmese hip hop.

The songs on *Sa-Tin-Chein* were not overtly political. But over time Zeyar Thaw went on to become a social activist, charity fundraiser and leading

Never Give Up
Generation Wave

GW never changes, we're never giving up
Failure's not a word we know. We fight till the bitter end
We won't be giving up, and every day that dawns
We won't be getting confused, we'll keep on going forward!
We're not just like a candle, goes out in a mild breeze
We're not a bunch of frogs, just sleeping under logs
Come and see.
Our group brings youth together
We'll keep on going down the path that we believe in, never weaken our resolve.
Stand up all of you, fight for your beliefs, march in step with the people.
We will never change, we and the people will never give up.
Failure's not a word we know, it's now certain that we'll fight till the bitter end
And every day that dawns, we won't be getting confused.

Young people open up your minds!
The time has come to dare to speak the truth!
Young people open up your minds!
The time has come to dare to speak the truth!
Build the courage to tell the truth.
The time has come to never give up.

Always blow air kisses at the one you do not like, tolerating the bullies, and never fighting back.
With an attitude like that, the people of Burma will never escape from the boot of the junta.
They'll dump their hated uniforms, they'll fake they're something else.
They stick elections 2010 in the headlines, think the people are dumb enough to buy it.
They should be so ashamed. They should fall down and die.
GW hey! GW hey!
These killers are adding insult to injury. We'll never give up!

http://www.globalpost.com/dispatch/asia/100511/myanmar-generation-wave

light of the underground youth organisation Generation Wave (GW). Prior to Generation Wave there was Myanmar Future Generation, a loose collective of young Burmese studying overseas who recorded pro-democracy rap songs and distributed them via their (now defunct) website. Set up during the 2007 Saffron Revolution, GW is trying to politicise a new generation of Burmese students through graffiti, slogans and pamphlets. At a time when the government was pushing for cars to switch to running on CNG (compressed natural gas), Zeyar Thaw created a sticker campaign with the slogan 'Change New Government'. He was arrested in March 2008 and sentenced to six years in November for forming an illegal organisation and illegally holding a small amount of foreign currency. He is being held in Kawthaung jail in Burma's far south.

The co-founder of ACID, Yan Yan Chan, was also detained for about nine months. Five other members of GW – Arkar Bo, Aung Zay Phyo, Thiha Win Tint, Wai Lwin Myo and Yan Naing Thu – were arrested with Zeyar Thaw at a restaurant and also sentenced to five years. At least ten GW members are thought to be behind bars. Before he was sentenced, Zeyar Thaw smuggled a statement out to GW members saying, 'Tell the people to have the courage to reject the things they don't like, and even if they don't dare to openly support the right thing, tell them not to support the wrong thing.'

Generation Wave uses music to further its cause and its supporters distribute songs with political messages from hand to hand. But not all GW members are musicians and not all of its music is hip hop. The music on the GW website http://www.gwave-network.co.cc/ is a mixture of political ballads, anthems and hip-hop songs with collages of photos, such as 'Mother 64', a 2009 birthday song for Aung San Suu Kyi, and 'Never Give Up'.

My Mandalay jail cellmate, Dr Hlaing Myint, was the father of one of the first generation hip-hop musicians, Bar-bu, who performed in a duo called Theory. He would often tell me his son was a hip-hop singer at a time when I wasn't sure what that was. The other member of Theory was Thxa Soe

Htein Lin's playlist

Yar Za Win Myar Ye Tha Doe Tha Mee (History's Bride)
Htoo Ein Thin

Sa Tin Chein (Beginning)
ACID

Alouq-jan-nehta-theq ta-chun
Killacash

145

Hip-hop performer Tun Tun at a concert in Rangoon, 25 September 2005
Credit: AFP/Getty Images

(pronounced 'Thar') who went on to study sound engineering in London. While he was there, he researched unknown 18th-century Burmese songs in the British Library and mixed them with his own – occasionally political – lyrics and hip-hop music. His 'Yawthama Hmwe' (Wooden Spoon Mix) became very popular, but by creating a hybrid of western and Burmese music he has now infringed the military government's desire for cultural purity. A recent Culture Ministry edict has banned the mixing of Burmese and western music. Thxa Soe has increasingly fallen foul of the censors, losing nine out of 12 songs from his most recent album, including 'Water, Electricity, Please Come Back'.

When I first heard hip hop in jail, like many others I could see the cultural links to Burmese *than-gyat*. *Than-gyat* is the call-and-response chants that we Burmese have been writing and performing each Burmese new year, accompanied by a drum beat. *Than-gyat* lyrics are topical, and traditionally include local grievances and exhortations to action. Unsurprisingly, since

1988, *than-gyat* of the sort I used to do in high school has not been allowed, but exiles still maintain the tradition. A Delhi group produces an annual CD, which is sold overseas and smuggled inside the country, or downloaded from the internet or broadcast by the Democratic Voice of Burma. The Delhi *than-gyat* group criticises the government and deals with topical issues such as forced labour, the military's nuclear ambitions and this year's upcoming elections. But the opposition and the exile movement are not immune from their barbs.

After my release from prison in November 2004, I met up with the leading comedian Zarganar, my old friend and mentor, who is now serving a 35-year jail sentence. I discovered his son, Myat Kaung, was part of the second generation of Burmese hip-hop artists, performing as Killacash. He is now in exile with his mother and sister, writing songs that are distributed on the internet. One song that became particularly notorious was 'Alouq-jan-neh ta-theq ta-chun' (Hard Labour for Life), about exile politics. Other famous second generation groups are J-Me, Ontrack, Cyclone, Chit Soe, Kyat Pha and Yatha, who combined with the members of ACID and Theory to form the Myanmar Hip Hop Association, which has been important in raising the profile of the genre across the country.

Nowadays, third generation hip-hop songs circulate as stage-show bootlegs and demos, recorded on increasingly accessible home equipment. Most of these songs are therefore going nowhere near official channels or the censors. There are live shows in Rangoon and Mandalay almost every week during the cool season, and videos are uploaded to sites such as http://burmesemtv.com/. Although some third generation bands have faced problems with the authorities, this is often because they like to swear and trade insults. One of the most notorious 3G rappers is Jauq Jeq (Baby's Rattle), whose gangsta-rap style sexist lyrics and videos have been heavily criticised online by Burmese women and provoked a formal warning from the Myanmar Music Association. While the advent of four state-run TV channels in Burma means that hip hop has more chance of getting shown, it can still be banned just because it uses informal pronouns for 'you' and 'I', like '*nin*' and '*nga*', perceived to be insulting to older viewers.

Problems with the authorities are seized upon hopefully by those outside the country as signs that hip hop inside Burma is becoming a vehicle for dissent. For example, exile news stories suggest that the group 9mm was only able to circulate songs 'underground' and never released an album because they were too political. The truth appears more mundane: according to another hip-hop artist their problem was that they couldn't afford a producer, and that their songs were mostly about girls. The one occasion they were banned was because a band member wore a terrorist mask on stage.

Cheap home studios and MP3s have led to the collapse of the previous system of censorship of music in Burma, just as blogging has broken down the control of news. But it doesn't follow that this has led to a vibrant political underground in Burma to take advantage of the opportunities. Groups based outside do their best to create a greater political awareness among Burma's young people. But inside the country, the circus of Burma's burgeoning 'yoof' culture, with stage shows, nightclubs and celebrity gossip, has all the scope to keep Burma's young people busy thinking about anything other than politics. Providing Burma's military can swallow their dislike of baggy jeans, sloppy pronouns and short skirts (many sported by their own well-heeled children), the regime may realise that pop and hip-hop music can be a harmless *tweq-pauq* or release valve for today's frustrated youth. ❐

© Htein Lin
39(3): 140/148
DOI: 10.1177/0306422010379805
www.indexoncensorship.org

Htein Lin is an artist and pioneer in performance art in Burma. He was imprisoned from 1998 to 2004 and now lives in London. His work has been exhibited in Thailand, Hong Kong, Bath (UK), London and Turin

Free Word Centre

Promoting literature, literacy
and free expression

'The transforming power of words'

Hire Our Space

Our beautiful hall can hold 200 people for
parties and events, or 90 for lectures and conferences.
Our bright and modern meeting rooms can hold
up to 18 people for meetings and workshops.
To book call: 020 7324 2570

Competitive rates for Associates
To find out more check out our website:
www.freewordonline.com
60 Farringdon Road, London, EC1R 3GA

TRADITION OF PROTEST

Performing political songs can lead to severe punishment in Tibet. **Woeser** celebrates a singer who is not afraid to confront taboos

Until 2008, I had never heard of Tibetan singer Tashi Dhondup. Like many others, I first became aware of him because of one particular song about the protests spreading through Tibet. It described not only 2008, but also 1958 – the entire five decades of Tibetan suffering. The lyrics were short, but each line was explosive. What other Tibetan singer within China's borders has sung so plainly?

> The year of 1958
> Is when the black enemy entered Tibet
> Is when the lamas were put in prison
> That time was terrifying ...
> The year of 2008
> Is when innocent Tibetans were beaten
> Is when people of the world were massacred
> That time was terrifying.

I listened over and over to that song, 'The Terror of 1958–2008'. The accompaniment Dhondup plays is crisp and pleasant, his voice full of painful memories and a desolation beyond his years – he is in his 20s. A friend of mine in Beijing, who is a musician, told me that he preferred Amdo and Kham to Lhasa when he visited Tibet, as he was enchanted by the mandolin-accompanied singers. He said that the mandolin – which originated in Italy – seemed to be more popular there than anywhere else in the world, with countless skilled Tibetan musicians. You hear it played not only in the countryside, but also by monks singing in monastery courtyards. Many fund their own simple recordings, a sign of real passion. The mandolin is now known by the Tibetan word *dranyen*, meaning guitar or lute, and instruments are decorated with bright local colours and motifs. Tibet has made the instrument its own.

Someone sent me a photo of Dhondup. Round-faced, with long narrow eyes, he appeared fashionable, dressed in black hunting gear with lightened hair. Apparently he used to sing songs of love and home: now that he was breaking the silence of a dark night, would he become a target for hunters? I heard that he was once detained and I would not have blamed him for opting to fall silent – falling silent at gunpoint is normal for us now, with many talented singers opting to stick to traditional songs and propaganda in exchange for fame. But Dhondup chose not to castrate himself that way – the next time he sang it was not one song, but 13. The album *Scarred Heart* sold 5,000 copies, selling out in many parts of Amdo. Tipped off that the police were preparing to arrest him for performance and distribution of 'reactionary songs', Dhondup fled his home. He had just got married. Several days later, the road-weary policemen caught up with him in a Xining hotpot restaurant as he was drinking with friends and detained him.

One of his relatives is a monk at a renowned lamasery. He has access to the internet and told me over Skype that the album was available online, with videos of Dhondup singing on mountaintops and grasslands. 'He looks great in Tibetan clothing, just like a star.' His admiring tone turned my sorrow into joy. I really wanted

Woeser's playlist

The Terror of 1958–2008
Tashi Dhondup
Available on vimeo.com

Grief
Genga
Available on YouTube

Chak Sum Tsel
Phurbu T Namgyal
Available on YouTube

to know what the lyrics meant, so we listened again several times as he explained, and the melodies travelled though limitless space to be heard by me, as if at a secret time we were burdened with the same fate. The lyrics brought tears to my eyes.

> I've never seen the Dalai Lama
> So I feel that I'm a poor Tibetan
> I didn't join the protest in 2008
> So I feel that I'm a useless Tibetan
> I didn't hoist the Snow Lion
> So I feel I'm useless even as a man.

The recordings banned in Tibet are of course not to be found in Beijing, but I could hear and see Dhondup online. Young Tibetan commentators praised him as an ethnic hero and applauded his courage. But as news of Dhondup reached the outside world and reports started to appear, the songs were deleted. At this point I met a Tibetan who had studied in India. It seemed as if he had appeared simply to translate the lyrics – I never heard from him again, very mysterious. He translated two songs into Chinese, and anyone hearing them could not fail to be moved. I noted down this passage:

> The sorrow that a man of the Holiness doesn't return home
> The sorrow that my fellow became separated
> The sorrow that freedom doesn't come to Tibet
> This is my pain without a wound ...

This is considered a reactionary song. I remember at the end of 2008 the deputy head of the Lhasa Public Security Bureau announced the arrest of 59 'rumour-mongers' for 'inciting ethnic sentiment'. These particular rumours were spread by 'illegally downloading reactionary songs, and selling them to the public on CD and as MP3 and MP4 files'. But this may confuse many – the concept of 'reactionary songs' is not a common one. It has its own unique meaning. As a Chinese commenter once said: 'Many ask what totalitarianism means, but it's like asking what rain means – it's hard to express, but you know when you're caught in it.' So when a *Times* reporter asked me what constituted a reactionary song, I could easily list at least ten. Perhaps she was only surprised by the strict ban on songs that merely mentioned our exiled spiritual leader. Straight-talkers like Tashi Dhondrup are rare, but he dared to sing:

> Your holiness Dalai Lama
> Please no longer be a wanderer
> There are many pious people in Tibet
> We are always waiting for you by the side of your throne.

Other reactionary songs are more oblique, using a white tower or golden sun to refer to the Dalai Lama.

If we view reactionary songs as a product of the past 50 years, it has clearly already become a tradition: a tradition of protest, a tradition of not submitting, a tradition that spreads endlessly. Many of these songs are written by Tibetans in exile, but also by those within China's borders – at all times and in every region, not just today or only in certain cities or villages. Some songs are blunt and immediately banned, some more subtle and so tacitly allowed to circulate. It would be an interesting topic for an academic study. But for us – that is, for my generation – memories of reactionary songs go back to the 1980s, such as these popular lyrics from 1989:

> We haven't bought India
> Nor sold Lhasa
> The Dalai Lama is not homeless
> The Norbulingka will be yet more splendid
> We Tibetans are looking forward
> And in one or two years
> We'll return in freedom

I've been told that normally servile Tibetan cadres from the local Academy of Sciences once got drunk at a festival celebration and choked back tears as they sang these words.

It seems normal to us now when the authorities stamp on reactionary songs. But only in Lhasa did they arrest as many as 59 at once for distributing music, and I heard they were mostly students. What was the purpose? Were they so angry at the popularity of these songs that a major arrest was necessary to serve as a lesson to the rest? Or could they not come up with any 'splittists' and had to make downloading a few songs of home and the Dalai Lama into a major crime? Or are those who rely on the 'anti-splittist' struggle for their living, creating enemies for the great Party?

Dhondup was swiftly punished – sentenced to 15 months of re-education through labour and sent back to his home village, once populated by nomadic herders. One day a Tibetan friend of mine, whom I hadn't seen for a long time, came to visit me. He is a fine poet in our native language and has travelled widely. But I had no idea he was also related to Dhondup. However, the Dhondup he spoke of was a wayward youth who liked to get drunk, sing, and chase grassland girls. At a meal to celebrate his release from detention for singing 'The Terror of 1958–2008', he even needed stitches after a drunken fight with a young Rimpoche (reincarnated Tibetan lama). Not without pride, my friend told me: 'He's a hero now. When I ask at roadside stalls in Xining if they've got his songs they make sure I'm not police or undercover, then pull out a big bag full of his recordings. They're all copies of course.' ❑

©Woeser
39(3): 150/155
DOI: 10.1177/0306422010380140
www.indexoncensorship.org

Woeser is an author and poet. Born in Lhasa, she is the author of *Notes on Tibet* (Huacheng Press), which is banned in China. She writes a blog and was one of the original signatories of Charter 08

TRANCE MUSIC

Zar's challenge to orthodox Islam poses a threat to its
survival. **Rachel Aspden** reports

Late on a Monday night in one of the hundreds of winding mud alleys of Cairo's Darb al Ahmar district, a middle-aged woman in a black robe and headscarf is welcoming friends to her one-room house. 'Salaam aleikum.' She offers an elbow in greeting rather than her hands, which are red to the wrists with fresh blood. Behind her, the turquoise-painted room is hung with round goatskin drums and rough handmade lyres decorated with beads and bright scraps of fabric. On the worn carpet is a shallow dish of blood half-submerging a clutter of gold rings and amulets: the remains of the animal sacrifice that begins the zar ritual.

Zar is a semi-secret musical ceremony for healing mental and physical illnesses its followers believe are caused by spirit possession. The ritual is practised throughout the Muslim communities of North and East Africa and the Arabian peninsula, almost exclusively by and for women. At its heart is a repertoire of thousands of magical songs and rhythms – each associated with a particular spirit that can cause or cure maladies ranging from depression to infertility, broken bones and heart disease. During a zar, women are free to cast off social constraints and behave as the spirit possessing them demands – to dance, sing, shout, weep and enter tranced states – even, sometimes, to dress in men's clothes, smoke hashish or drink alcohol.

Inside the room – the home of Leila, the zar leader – eight 40- to 60-year-old women in long flowered gowns and headscarves have gathered on cushions along the walls, smoking waterpipes and drinking glasses of sugary tea. Darb al Ahmar is a poor working-class district and their faces are lined with hard work and worry. As the ritual begins, Leila's assistant carries round a small brazier smouldering with heavy incense and, muttering prayers and blessings, douses each woman in its smoke. In return, each offers 30LE (£3.50) – a significant sum – to pay the musicians and cover the cost of the incense and sacrificial chickens.

Then three musicians strike up the opening music of the ceremony, their voices rising roughly over the thunder of their drums. In the tiny room, the sound is wild and overwhelming, designed to entice the spirits and intoxicate the participants. As each woman hears the rhythm associated with 'her' spirit, she is drawn up to dance in the centre of the room, a blood-spotted white veil thrown over her head and face, before collapsing exhausted to the ground. The spirit is pacified – for the moment. 'This is when the healing takes place,' Leila explains later. 'When we are all gathered together to help to focus on the patient.'

Rachel Aspden's playlist

Ahlan Be Eltlat Asyad
Rango
30 IPS

Yousef Madala
Awlad Abu al Gheit
Available on iTunes

Afrah
El Tanbura
30 IPS

Despite their social benefits, zar gatherings are increasingly rare. This is partly due to changing fashions – the ritual, which arrived in Egypt with Sudanese slaves in the early 19th century, is seen as too old-fashioned and *baladi* ('country') for a modern urban environment. But it is also the result of a religious reaction against zar's heterogeneous roots in Islam, Christianity and African animism. The spirits it summons include the Prophet and familiar Islamic figures such as his granddaughter Sayyida Zeinab, Cairo's patron saint – alongside Christian, Ottoman, western and pagan figures such as Yawra Bey, a cigar-smoking, whiskey-sipping dandy, and Mariam, the sister of a Coptic Christian priest, who is part mournful lady, part whore. Zar's blurring of doctrinal boundaries – the figure of al Araby, for instance, a Bedouin nomad who leads a camel, blends into that of Mohammed – is anathema to the increasingly conservative Islamic mainstream.

In the Suez Canal city of Port Said, I visit Sheikha Zeinab, a motherly 65-year-old zar leader, and her musicians Araby Jacomo and Awad. 'Thirty years ago, people respected zar,' she explains, handing round glasses of 7-Up in her tiny cluttered living room. 'But in the last few years, Egyptians have grown more closed-minded and fanatical.' The musicians fear that the influence of religious satellite TV channels such as al Rahma, whose charismatic tele-sheikhs regularly fulminate against zar, and the proliferation of Islamic guidance websites may drive the ritual and its music to extinction. 'Zar is based on superstition and the belief in devils,' admonishes a fatwa (Islamic legal opinion) on the Egypt-based website IslamOnline. 'Islam is totally against it, and it is just a kind of delusion and deception.' Until the government moved to suppress extremist groups in the noughties, zar sessions in Port Said were frequently disrupted by threatening visits from 'the bearded ones' – local Islamist vigilantes.

Even the zar musicians disagree on its orthodoxy. 'It is completely Islamic – we sing to the prophet and his companions. There is nothing against zar in the Quran,' says Araby Jacomo defensively. But the sheikha is prepared to disagree. 'It's not Islamic – it draws on Islamic elements,' she says. 'It is something more open than any one religion.' It is this open and accepting quality, she believes, that can attract even the most religious to it. 'People who have problems started to follow the religious scholars on TV rather than the zar,' says Sheikha Zeinab. 'But when they have a problem caused by the spirits, they call the TV channels' freephone hotlines or go to medical doctors, who can't cure it. They spend so much time and money searching for a cure, and finally they come back to zar, even if they don't want to believe in it.'

The hostility to zar reflects an unease with music and dance – especially where women are concerned – that dates back to the earliest days of Islam. For centuries, scholars have debated the ground between the 'purest' form of music – the call to prayer and recitation of the Quran – and lesser or forbidden forms. The 12th-century theologian al Ghazali famously warned against the disruptive power of music. 'The heart of man has been so constituted by the Almighty that, like a flint, it contains a hidden fire which is evoked by music and harmony, and renders man beside himself with ecstasy,' he wrote. At different times, the percussion, stringed instruments and dancing of zar have all been considered un-Islamic – as has women's singing. '*Sawt al mar'a awra*' states a famous proverb: 'a woman's voice is a shameful thing'.

But as well as providing women with a rare opportunity to escape the pressures of a conservative society, the zar repertoire tells the story of Egypt's last 200 years. Its songs and the spirits they invoke even hold a mirror up to the changes that threaten its own survival, explains Hager el Hadidi, an anthropologist who has been a zar participant herself for the last decade. 'With the Islamic revival, the Muslim zar spirits – the prophet and his companions and family – are beginning to dominate the rest,' she says. The Jewish spirits that were prominent in zar songs of the 40s and 50s – reflecting Cairo's then-thriving Jewish community – have disappeared. Their place is being taken by Christian spirits associated with western consumer goods such as freezers and plasma-screen TVs, and new songs adapted from soap opera theme-tunes. 'As society becomes increasingly concerned with maintaining the appearance of piety, it's easy to sacrifice zar, which is something marginal,' says al Hadidi. But if zar vanishes, an irreplaceable piece of Egypt's history will be lost. ❐

©Rachel Aspden
39(3): 156/160
DOI: 10.1177/0306422010381166
www.indexoncensorship.org

Rachel Aspden is a Winston Churchill Memorial Trust travelling fellow, writing on culture and Islam

NEW FROM SAQI BOOKS

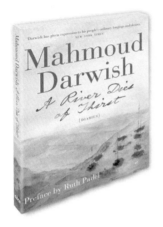

'Darwish speaks of the fight to keep love and vision alive in a world overshadowed by the military-industrial complex, and, as such, is deeply relevant to us all.' *Daily Mail*

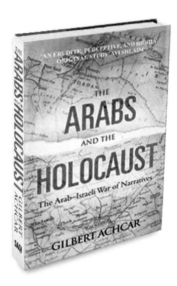

'A work of breath-taking empathy... [A] magisterial study' **Rashid Khalidi**

'Essential reading for anyone who seeks a balanced understanding of the place of Jews and the Holocaust in Arab thinking today.' **Michael R. Marrus**

'A jewel of a memoir' **Maureen Freely**

'Moving and remarkable' **Andrew Finkel**

CONTROL SHIFT

Cuban musicians and artists are pushing the boundaries and challenging the status quo. **Jan Fairley** interprets the counterpoint of free speech and censorship

April 2010 and Havana's Teatro Acapulco, a large, old 1,500 seat auditorium, is full to bursting, with another probable 1,000 people outside listening in as leading Cuban hip-hop group Los Aldeanos open their gig with the song 'Censurado' (Censored). The message of this event is ambiguous and the central question arising from it is: what does it mean to invoke the idea of censorship if one is free to sing about it to a live audience? Indeed, Los Aldeanos were not just free to sing about censorship, freedom and other issues but their concert was organised by Asociación Hermanos Saíz, the cultural arm of Cuba's young communist movement, so there is no doubt that it had been sanctioned at the highest level.

And yet only a year ago, for a specific period from about May 1999 until January 2010, it was difficult to hear Los Aldeanos play live in Cuba. The fact that some of their songs challenge the status quo had led to harassment and proscription by the authorities. However, as was shown in the late 1990s, when timba-dance group La Charanga Habanera was grounded after a controversial high-profile performance televised to an international audience, such 'banning' can actually increase the popularity of an already popular

Revolution Square during the Paz Sin Fronteras (Peace without Borders) *concert, Havana*
21 September 2009
Credit: Reuters/Pool

group. In 2010, any notion of 'control' is harder to effect: over the past 15 years Cuba has seen the extensive, unofficial, inflow of technology that has enabled the creation and production of music and its informal distribution in various digital formats, from CD to DVD to MP3. The idea that any state can control culture through the media grows ever more tenuous, particularly as the media itself is subject to the editorial judgment and self-censorship of those who work for it, whose taste is liable to be influenced by new innovations and trends.

The issue of freedom of speech became more contested in Cuba in the 'Special Period' of the 1990s, when dramatic economic, ideological and political shifts saw a whole set of changes, including the influx of new tourists to the island, which fuelled the flow and availability of digital technology. This had an impact on creativity, home recording possibilities, music distribution and the diversity of the music scene, as research by a number of academics has shown (see below for further reading). Since the 1997 appointment of poet and writer Abel Prieto as minister of culture, Cuba has witnessed a further freeing up of the cultural scene and more open debate.

The most recent notable case of music censorship in Cuba is that of Gorki Águila, leader of the group Porno Para Ricardo, championed by Freemuse and Index on Censorship. It revolved around Águila's 2003 sentence to four years' imprisonment for alleged amphetamine drug trafficking at a Pinar del Río rock festival. Internationally it was asserted that the drug allegation was a pretext to silence Águila and Porno Para Ricardo's punk-orientated rock music. Their provocative lyrics coupled with the band's anarchic sensibilities, with outspoken attacks on communism, all sorts of officialdom and other political and cultural targets, led to Águila's sentence being interpreted as punishment for his music. After a year in a provincial prison, Águila was transferred to an open prison in Havana, where he reportedly joined the prison salsa band and was required to teach music to fellow inmates. He was released in 2005 after two years' imprisonment, and took up a day job at the Instituto Cubano de Artes e Industrias Cinematograficas (ICAIC) film studios.

While acknowledging that Porno Para Ricardo's lyrics and performances may be interpreted as 'provocative', it can also be argued that Águila's case is an exceptional, if not isolated, incident; not typical of the way matters around censorship and self-censorship are handled in Cuba today. To understand Cuba it is necessary to see the role that artists have played in pushing the envelope of what is permitted. Trying to gauge censorship in Cuba just by listening to anti-Castro rhetoric (in a 2007 interview with CNN, post-imprisonment, Águila called communism 'a failure') does not produce an accurate picture. As in many countries, artists of all kinds have preferred to fight for change from within rather than without, and Cuba is no exception.

Los Aldeanos have a number of songs in their repertoire that challenge the status quo. They not only address hot subjects debated officially and unofficially, such as freedom of speech and expression, but also as their name (The Villagers) suggests, more subtle issues of social inequality which are a stressful fact of everyday life for Cubans, yet rarely dealt with by the Cuban media. As such, their songs join a number of others written since the 1960s which function as barometers of what people on the street in Cuba are think-ing and discussing about the impact of government decisions on their lives.

Los Aldeanos have suffered various instances of what Martin Cloonan has called 'prior restriction' and 'suppression' in his pioneering work defining the complexities of censorship within different political and economic systems. They have had their laptop seized temporarily in a country where possession and provenance of technology can leave Cubans vulnerable to official query. While this situation may be used as a form of control, most often the authorities concerned (customs and excise, the police) turn a blind eye to provenance and use. And many artists who have imported technology legitimately have full permission to use it. Still, such major Cuban musicians as Cándido Fabré have sung about the intimidation and behaviour of the Holguin airport customs in seizing excessive goods from Cubans returning home to the island.

Live shows have always seen musicians and other artists freely impro-vising and singing lyrics which directly or ironically could be seen to be criticising the status quo, as in the case of Los Aldeanos' Havana perform-ance. This became particularly acute during the vibrant, cultural scene of the Special Period of the 1990s, when Cuba's rapid economic transformation saw the new tourism equated with a hedonistic scene. Indeed, throughout this period timba musicians in particular commented succinctly and wit-tily about changes in social behaviour, often referring to the new informal *jinetera* 'service' industry. Dance bands pushed the envelope of ironic com-ment and various rock musicians and singer-songwriters complained about certain songs not being played on the radio due to direct censorship or an editorial policy unduly influenced by considerations of what might cause offence to the authorities.

Rock-troubadour Carlos Varela has declared that while able to sing cer-tain songs live, they were never played on the radio or television. These include 'Guillermo Tell', which asks William Tell's father when he will swap

Salsa group La Charanga Habenera, Cuba, October 1997
Credit: Ernesto Bazan/Liaison/Getty Images

roles and allow his son a chance to try to shoot the apple off *his* head. At the height of the tragic exodus and death of many Cubans trying to escape the harshness of the Special Period by sailing to the US in unsafe homemade rafts, Varela wrote 'Robinson', the story of a man who found himself abandoned on an island. Among other songs about exile and loss, Varela wrote 'Fotos de Familia', in which he conjures up an absent diaspora found only in photographs.

High-profile, innovative groups such as NG La Banda, founded by José Luís Cortés, composed topical songs about subjects such as the street sale of scarce foodstuffs like beef, acquired illegally, and the distribution of soya in rations rather than fish on an island surrounded by sea. Cortés was brought to task by the Women's Federation for his song 'La Bruja' (The Witch), which implicitly referenced Cuban women who had relationships with non-Cuban tourists. In 1997, top dance band La Charanga Habanera were grounded and later forced to publicly re-examine their behaviour after they had headlined the final concert of the 14th World Festival of Youth and Students. In a wild performance broadcast live on Cuban television with international crews also present, among many things they allegedly boasted about drugs and invited the local audience to further internationalism by jumping the crash barriers that lay between them and their guests. Previously they had composed various controversial songs including a subversive re-working of 'Tengo', an iconic poem by acclaimed Afro-Cuban poet Nicolas Guillen, and 'El Mango', whose lyrics asked when the big green mango would fall from the tree (taken as alluding to Fidel Castro).

Wit, irony and double entendre of a political, as well as the more characteristic sexual type, underscore the 'transgressive' nature of such songs. They show the limits of freedom of expression (which in La Charanga Habanera's case might have passed without note if the performance had not been broadcast live) are focused on publicly indulging in behaviour that could bring the island's culture into disrepute by referring to drug taking and, more subtly, challenging the government's 'best efforts' by highlighting social contradictions. Acts of restriction or suppression can, it seems, be ideologically determined, arising when themes have been deemed to challenge the 'best interests' of Cuban society.

Perhaps the clearest message that many Cubans are fighting against censorship and self-censorship internally came early in 2010 at the Havana Book Fair, which this year was dedicated to poet, essayist and narrator César López. At the start of the fair, López read a criticism of the homophobia and repressive acts that were directed against various writers toward the end of the 1960s and the beginning of the 1970s. In January, just before the book fair, three programmes were shown on Cuban television celebrating the contribution of what were described as three key figures, making it appear as if they had made valuable contributions to Cuban culture in the 1960s and early 1970s: Luis Pavón Tamayo, who directed the Council on National Culture (today the Ministry of Culture); Jorge Serguera, who presided over the Cuban Institute of Radio and Television (ICRT) and was linked to the 'revolutionary trials' against those opposing the state; and Armando Quesada, who took charge of theatre in the country. The programmes drew an immediate angry response from writers and artists on the island at the apparent vindication of what they described as three 'executioners'.

Debate began on the internet, via email, blogs and different forums, culminating in a large meeting at Cuba's intellectual powerhouse, the Casa de las Américas, the country's emblematic institution of artistic culture. In an interview with Arturo García Hernández, for Mexico's *La Jornada* in February,

Cuba's culture minister, Abel Prieto (former president of UNEAC, the Cuban National Union of Writers and Artists), reported that after an outcry against the programmes by intellectuals on the island, a series of discussions took place at UNEAC headquarters. In Prieto's words, 'The [Communist] Party leadership sent them a message, of which I was the bearer, to explain that there had been an error in presenting these three former officials on television. Why? Because today the leadership of this country regards that period – which was fortunately brief – with great disapproval, where we set aside the cultural policies that the revolution implemented in 1961 in which we brought together the cultural work of artists and writers of all tendencies, of all generations – Catholic, communist, even non-revolutionaries who were sincere.'

Prieto then reclarified Fidel Castro's famous 1961 words to intellectuals – 'inside the revolution everything, outside the revolution nothing' – for the 21st century: 'That is a moment, a phrase, inside the speech "*Palabras a los intelectuales*". What happens is that when you take it out [of context] it becomes a slogan, and people say OK, but who interprets what is or is not within the revolution? Fidel himself says that even within the revolution there has to be a space to work within culture for those intellectuals who are not themselves revolutionary. That is to say, [working] within does not mean exclusion, rather a call to the broadest range of tendencies.'

The period between 1971 and 1976 is now officially recognised in Cuba as the 'Grey Five' years due to episodes of censorship and repression. It is obvious from a close reading of accounts that this period saw internal conflict between bureaucrats and artists as to how revolutionary culture should be defined, specifically challenges to ideas of socialist realism and propaganda. In fact the official dates of 1971–6 need to be extended further back to the mid-1960s: in 1966 a young singer, Pablo Milanés, while doing obligatory military service, was incarcerated along with others – some for homosexuality, others for 'bohemianism' – in a UMAP (Unidad Militar de Ayuda a la Producción) or forced labour camp, in the countryside

Jan Fairley's playlist

Ojalá (Let's Hope/ God Willing)
Silvio Rodríguez

Guillermo Tell (William Tell)
Carlos Varela

Niñito Cubano (Cuban Child)
Los Aldeanos

near Camagüey in central Cuba. At the time, the existence of this UMAP camp was challenged by many artists and intellectuals. Milanés's case was championed by various key figures, including singers such as Elena Burke and Omara Portuondo, film-maker Estela Bravo and significantly by Haydée Santamaría, one of those who had fought with Fidel Castro, Ché Guevara and other guerrillas in the Sierra Maestra and who was founding director of the Casa de las Américas.

Milanés's imprisonment was first publicly acknowledged in Tomás Gutiérrez Alea and Juan Carlos Tabío's 1994 Cuban-Mexican film *Fresa y Chocolate* (Strawberry and Chocolate), based on Senal Paz's short story *El lobo, el bosque y el hombre nuevo* (The Wolf, the Forest and the New Man). At the time, Casa de las Américas was involved in the organisation of OLAS (Organización Latinoamericana de Solidaridad), known by its acronym which means 'waves', a series of bi-lateral meetings intended to make waves by moving Cuba out of its Cold War isolation through exchange with Latin America and other countries. As part of OLAS, Casa de las Américas organised the seminal 1967 Encuentro de la Canción Protesta (protest song meeting).

So while Milanés was in a UMAP, musicians including singers from the UK, France, Italy and Spain, the US and the Americas were giving concerts, exchanging ideas, discussing creativity and what role, if any, music might play in the struggle for socialism. Upon his release the same year, Milanés was invited to join the Centro de la Canción Protesta, founded after the Encuentro protest meeting by Santamaria at Casa de las Américas. At the end of 1969, with the support of notably Santamaría and Alfredo Guevara, one of the founders and president of the Instituto Cubano de Artes e Industrias Cinematograficas (ICAIC) who had both fought for the revolution and were members of inner revolutionary circles, Milanés joined Silvio Rodríguez as a member of the newly formed Grupo Experimental Sonora de ICAIC (GESI), composing soundtracks for new ICAIC films. Singer-songwriter Rodríguez had hosted a music television programme for a time until he fell out of favour with a Cuban Institute of Radio and Television (ICRT) bureaucrat and it was taken off air.

Over time, GESI members became part of the nascent *nueva trova* movement, supported by the island-wide infrastructure provided by the same Hermanos Saenz cultural organisation that has been supporting Los Aldeanos. Over a number of years the joke was that the songs of Rodríguez and Milanés went from being 'banned to obligatory': indeed, their songs became the seminal soundscape of the Spanish-speaking world in the 70s and 80s through a host of networks that constellated during the fight for freedom in Nicaragua and El Salvador and the dark period of military dictatorships in Latin America, which saw the end of the Franco period in Spain. To understand their massive popularity as mere appropriation by the state is not only to misunderstand cultural struggle and power structures within Cuba but also to ignore the 'zeitgeist' poetic power of their music.

So while there have been cases of censorship in Cuba, focusing on them alone can blind one to the active work to define revolutionary politics by artists themselves. One key factor in understanding contemporary cultural policy is encompassed by the figure of poet and writer Prieto himself: he was part of the 60s generation, along with Rodríguez and Milanés, who fought to establish their own spaces from the margins. Prieto's appointment in 1997 as minister of culture was a strong sign of opening up and a re-evaluation of the significance of the 60s period. Faithful to his long-haired style, Prieto recognised rock and rap as authentic forms of Cuban artistic expression soon after taking office.

The 20 September 2009 Paz Sin Fronteras (Peace without Borders) concert in Revolution Square, which drew a live audience of more than a million, as well as a massive continental television audience of many millions more, has pushed barriers further. True, like the 2001 visit of the Manic Street Preachers, it also functioned as an opportunity for the Cuban authorities to show they could cope with non-Cuban stars singing messages to the Cuban people, but this time the message was not about Cuba versus the US, but about building bridges and peace. Organised by Colombian music star Juanes, with the help of Silvio Rodríguez and the Cuban Ministry of Culture, it is notable that Juanes is the only person other than Pope John Paul II to be given permission to entertain the Cuban people and the world from the same place, Revolution Square.

Juanes organised the first Paz Sin Fronteras concert in March 2008 on the Simón Bolívar Bridge linking Colombia and Venezuela to promote peace after a diplomatic crisis there almost led to armed conflict. The aim of the second event, under the iconic gaze of Ché Guevara and the statue of revolutionary intellectual José Martí, was to further the idea of a thaw in US-Cuban relations through the diplomacy of music, with a loud call for 'One Cuban family'.

With a top rosta of Latin stars dressed in white in the name of peace, the Havana concert officially 'had nothing to do with politics or ideology'. Yet the fact that a 17 Latin Grammy award-winning artist had been given Cuban government permission and support to organise such an

Rap group Los Aldeanos performing at Teatro Acapulco, Havana, 23 April 2010
Credit: AFP/Getty Images

event focused everyone's mind on the key question of whether music can help break the 50-year US blockade and stalemate in the US-Cuban relationship.

While the feeling of the concert was pro-Cuban, it was by no means uncritical. Over a million Cubans and others living on the island (notably international students from practically every Latin American country) came and stood in the intense heat to enjoy the music and interpret songs in various ways. Puerto Rico's charismatic Olga Tañón, the only major female figure, opened her set of merengues with 'Basta Ya' (That's Enough), playing to an almost word-perfect crowd.

Cuban rocker X-Alfonso raised the emotional stakes with a thundering version of 'Revolución' alongside his parents (of seminal Afro-Cuban group Sintesis) and a children's gospel choir. His group's female rapper sang potentially subversive lines like 'down with control'. Carlos Varela, the only artist dressed in black, happily sang 'Muro' (Wall), which speaks of longing for a world outside Cuba's Malecón seawall, and his searing '25 Mil Mentiras sobre la Verdad' (Twenty-five Thousand Lies about Truth).

Spanish veterans Víctor Manuel and Luís Eduardo Aute, who held the flame of freedom during the Franco years, sang emblematic songs against dictatorship. Italy's Jovanotti threw lines from Bob Marley's 'Get Up, Stand Up' into 'Umbilical of the World'. Juanes, who had received death threats via Twitter from Miami-Cuban hardliners who publicly destroyed the CDs of artists involved in the concert, sang his song for migrant workers, 'A Díos le Pidó' (I Ask God). Before singing 'No Creo en el Jamás' (I Don't Believe in Never) he told the crowd, 'The future is in your hands', and then dedicated 'Sueños' (Dreams), his song for Colombian kidnap victims, to all 'imprisoned unjustly or who seek freedom'. With Spanish singer Miguel Bosé, Juanes sang, 'It's Time to Change', telling the audience, 'We have overcome fear to be with you and we hope you too can overcome it.'

Silvio Rodríguez sang his classic 60s song 'Ojalá', which means 'God Willing', shouting 'Viva el pueblo Cubano!' In his farewell address, Juanes namechecked Los Aldeanos, whom he had wanted to invite to sing at the concert. That same week the security forces, on alert because of the unique nature of the concert coupled with threats from Miami, took Los Aldeanos into custody and seized their laptop, only to free them and later return it. It is said that Silvio Rodríguez intervened on their behalf. Since then, Pablo Milanés has sung with them at La Piragua, the open-air performance space on the Malecón outside the US Interests Section.

So those who in the 60s were subject to 'prior restraint', suppression and punishment have in turn supported a new generation of artists and continue to strive for freedom of expression on the island. That this is expressed within the revolutionary ideological parameters is unsurprising, as that is the system of the country. Censorship in Cuba is as complex as it is in the rest of the world and musicians there are engaged with the political reality and taking risks in expressing its contradictions. Certainly in the creative climate that thrives there, despite scarce resources and many other considerations, the situation is much more subtle than being for or against the state. That 2010 is different to the 1960s may be as much due to technological innovation and changing contexts as it is to inter-generational dynamics.

The key relationship lies between the rights of the individual vis-a-vis collective rights within the ideological paradigms: that is, who decides what is in the collective interest and how that is decided. I would suggest that the liberally used term 'authorities' itself needs unpicking: there is no evidence of any monolithic single authority in Cuba making decisions on censorship. It is important, therefore, to distinguish between the balance of power and dialogue that exists between the Ministry of Culture, other parts of government, and other key professional groups such as the Union of Artists and Writers (UNEAC) and the legal frameworks within which the police and security forces work. In addition, it is important to be aware of differences of perspective, debate and tension that may arise inside these organisations in line with most other parts of the world. ❏

With thanks to Geoff Baker, Martin Cloonan and Alexandrine Fournier

©Jan Fairley
39(3): 162/173
DOI: 10.1177/0306422010380364
www.indexoncensorship.org

Further reading:
Martin Cloonan and Reebee Garofalo, *Policing Pop*, Temple University Press
Jan Fairley, '"Ay Dios Ampárame" (O God Protect Me): Music in Cuba during the 1990s, the Special Period', in K. Dawe (ed.), *Island Musics*, Berg
Vincenzo Perna, *Timba: The Sound of the Cuban Crisis*, Ashgate
Robin Moore, *Music and Revolution: Cultural Change in Socialist Cuba*, University of California Press
Ariana Hernández-Reguant (ed.) *Cuba in the Special Period: Culture and Ideology in the 1990s*, Palgrave Macmillan
Geoffrey Baker, 'The Politics of Dancing: Reggaetón and Rap in Havana, Cuba', in R. Rivera et al., *Reggaeton*, Duke University Press
Jan Fairley and Alexandrine Fournier 'Recording the Revolution', in Simon Frith and Simon Zagorski-Thomas, *The Art of Music Production* (forthcoming)

Jan Fairley is an ethnomusicologist and Latin American specialist. She has been researching Cuba since 1978. www.janfairley.com

A censorship chronicle incorporating information from Agence France-Presse (AFP), allAfrica, al Arabiya, ARTICLE 19 (A19), Asbarez, Bianet, British Broadcasting Corporation (BBC), Bloomberg, Burma News International, Committee to Protect Journalists (CPJ), Canadian Broadcasting Corporation (CBC), Caribbean e-News, *El Colombiano*, Freemuse, Gilgamesh Center for Kurdish Studies and Research, the *Global Post*, the *Guardian*, the *Herald Sun*, the *Independent*, the International Press Institute, the Irrawaddy, the *Jakarta Post*, the *Jamaica Observer*, journalism.co.za, Journaliste en Danger (JED), Kurdnet, Medialine News Agency, Menassat, the National Union of Somalian Journalists (NUSOJ), *New Music Express* (NME), the *New York Times*, the *Phnom Penh Post*, *Politiken*, Radio Free Asia, Reporters Sans Frontières (RSF), Reuters, Shortnews.com, Spinearth.tv, the *Straits Times*, the *St Petersburg Times*, the *Sydney Morning Herald* and other organisations affiliated with the International Freedom of Expression Exchange (IFEX)

Afghanistan

Singer **Shakib Mosadeq** and two members of his band were forced to leave the country in May 2010. Many of Mosadeq's songs address controversial subjects including corruption, fraud and human rights abuses. After the Afghan media refused to broadcast his music, he uploaded his songs to YouTube. His wife and daughter also fled the country at the same time. (Freemuse, *Global Post*)

On 23 March 2009, the attorney general's office arrested **Fahim Kohdamani**, manager of Amroz TV, for allegedly broadcasting 'anti-Islamic' and 'vulgar' content on his music programme *Biya wa Bibin*. The arrest followed the receipt of a letter from the Media Complaints Commission, accusing Amroz TV of broadcasting music that was detrimental to Afghan culture. (Freemuse, RSF)

Australia

Gold Coast residents called for the ban of a music festival promoting white supremacy and featuring neo-Nazi bands after posters and leaflets advertising the event were distributed throughout the city. The mayor said the council did not have authority to stop the **Hammered festival**, which took place on 17 April 2010 at a secret location. Although legal experts thought there might be a case for stopping the festival under the country's Racial Discrimination Act, both the mayor and community groups felt ignoring the event was the best way to deal with the situation. (Freemuse, *Sydney Morning Herald*)

Burma

In April 2010, the junta banned most of the songs on hip hop artist **Thxa Soe**'s album *Yaw Tal Hmway Tal* (Able to Mix and Blend). One of the songs banned was entitled 'Water, electricity, please come back'. Soe is hugely popular with the country's younger generation, and as a result he is watched closely by censorship officers and his concerts are attended by large numbers of security force personnel. (Freemuse, *Guardian*)

The Ministry of Culture outlawed the use of western musical instruments in the country's traditional **Saing orchestras** on 29 December 2009. Instructions were issued to the **Central Theatrical Association** and the 47 Saing orchestras in Mandalay division. The regulations also require Saing orchestra performers to wear traditional clothes. Disco strobe lighting and loudspeakers did not fall foul of the new ruling and were tolerated. (Freemuse, Irrawaddy)

Singer **Nyi Paing** and songwriter **Min Satta** were arrested on 16 October 2009. The arrests were part of a larger crackdown on those considered to be speaking out against the junta, which included journalists, human rights workers, monks, artists and student groups. Neither Satta's nor Paing's families were given any details of where they were being held or for how long. (A19, the Assistance Association for Political Prisoners in Burma, Freemuse, Irrawaddy)

Singer **Htoo Htoo Chay** was imprisoned on 13 September 2009. Following his release in October, he claimed that he had been tortured while in custody. (Burma News International, Freemuse)

Cambodia

On 18 March 2009, the Ministry of Culture and Fine Arts banned all music considered to be 'rude or obscene'. The prohibition prevents vendors, musicians, artists and comedians from selling, producing, singing or playing offensive songs. Five songs were immediately banned under the ruling, which was implemented to protect the country's cultural heritage. The minister for women's affairs also stated that the censorship could reduce violent crimes against women. (Freemuse, *Phnom Penh Post*)

Cameroon

The three-year prison sentence imposed on popular singer **Lapiro de Mbango** was upheld by an appeal court on 24 June 2009. Mbango, an outspoken government critic, was originally convicted on 24 September 2008 for allegedly participating in anti-government riots. His songs attack government corruption, and his 2008 'Constitution Constipée', banned from television and radio, attacked amendments to the constitution. (Freemuse, Writers in Prison Committee)

Chile

After almost 36 years, the former army conscript José Adolfo Paredes Márquez confessed to the killing of renowned folk singer **Victor Jara** on 27 May 2009. Jara had been tortured, with his hands shattered by rifle butts to prevent him playing guitar, before being shot 44 times in 1973. His death became a symbol of the gross human rights violations committed by Chilean authorities during General Pinochet's military dictatorship. (*Guardian*)

China

In April 2010, American singer **Bob Dylan** cancelled a tour of east Asia after the government allegedly refused permission for him to perform in Beijing and Shanghai. According to Dylan's tour promoter, the Ministry of Culture blocked the proposed concerts because of the singer's reputation as a protest singer and a counter-culture icon. (Freemuse, *Guardian*)

On 5 January 2010, authorities sentenced Tibetan singer **Tashi Dhondup** to 15 months' 're-education' for recording 'subversive songs' and for taking part in 'separatist activities'. The case did not go to trial and Dhondup's sentence was handed down by a municipal committee. The songs, about the Dalai Lama and the Chinese government's crackdown on Tibetans in March 2008, feature on banned album *Torture without Trace*, released in November 2009. Dhondup was arrested on 3 December 2009 and had been previously detained in September 2008. (Freemuse, *NME*, Radio Free Asia)

On 3 September 2009, the Ministry of Culture announced that all songs must obtain prior approval and be translated into Chinese before being uploaded to music websites. The move, officially designed to protect Chinese culture and intellectual property rights, obliges online music distributers such as **Yahoo China**, **Baidu** and **Google** to submit music to officials who will determine if it is 'acceptable'. A free internet music download service launched in April 2009, but banned songs were not made available via the service. (AFP, Freemuse, *Independent*)

Colombia

On 24 August 2009, civic leader and hip hop artist **Pacheco** was murdered in the western city of Medellín. An investigation was set up by local prosecutors to establish a motive for the killing of the 24-year-old vocalist of group C4. (*El Colombiano*, Indymedia)

Cuba

Vocalist **Aldo Roberto Rodríguez Baquero**, known as **El Aldeano** or **AL2**, was arrested on 28 September 2009. The singer of popular rap group Los Aldeanos has written numerous songs criticising Fidel Castro's regime, emphasising the need to end political, economic and social repression and 'tourism apartheid'. He was released the same day, although personal belongings, including his home computer, were confiscated. (Freemuse, LaJauretsi, MySpace)

On 20 August 2009, Colombian singer **Juanes** announced that he had received a series of death threats ahead of the Peace without Borders concert in Havana. The 20 September 2009 event was organised and headlined by the performer. Despite Juanes's stated intent to use the concert to promote unity, he faced criticism for including performers who support the Castro regime. Threats were issued via Twitter and a group of protesters gathered outside his home in Florida. (*Guardian*, Justnews.com)

Czech Republic

Scottish rock band **Primal Scream** were accused of 'promoting fascism' by the Czech Radio Council in March 2009. The accusations relate to the song 'Swastika Eyes', released in 2000, which was subsequently banned. Defenders of the band, who are known for their left-wing, anti-authoritarian politics, accused the council of misinterpreting the song's anti-fascist intent. (Freemuse, *Spin*)

Democratic Republic of Congo

The mayor of Likasi closed down **Community Radio of Katanga** and **Radiotelevision Likasi 4** on 11 March 2009. They were accused of playing music with emotional and political impact and of inciting violence after they broadcast a speech by the first prime minister of independent Congo. (CPJ, JED)

Denmark

A Social Democrat councillor unsuccessfully attempted to ban reggae artist **Sizzla** from performing in Copenhagen because of his anti-homosexual views. Although Sizzla signed the Reggae Compassionate Act, a promise to refrain from using homophobic language in music or live performances, campaigners have expressed concerns that the singer only signed the agreement to continue performing in Europe. The concert, which was council-funded, took place on 19 October 2009, with no reported homophobic remarks. (Freemuse, *Politiken*)

Egypt

Elton John was barred from playing at Egypt's Musician Union on 18 May 2010 because of his 'anti-religious beliefs'. Head of the Union, Mounir al Wasimi, cited the singer's homosexuality, anti-religious sentiments and outspoken comments about sexual freedom in the Middle East as reasons for the ban. (*Herald Sun*)

Ethiopia

On 13 August 2009, reggae singer **Teddy Afro** was released early from an Addis Ababa prison after serving 16 months of his six-year sentence. Hundreds of fans gathered to protest when the pop star, whose real name is Tewodros Kassahun, was originally sentenced in 2008 for killing a homeless man in a hit-and-run accident. He maintains his innocence and his supporters claim that the conviction was politically motivated because of his anti-government lyrics. (CBC News, Freemuse)

France

Normandy rapper **Orselsan** sparked a censorship row in July 2009 when he was removed from the Francofolies music festival line-up in La Rochelle. Dubbed the 'French Eminem', Orselsan's violent and sexist lyrics have made him a controversial figure in France. Organisers claimed that his omission was instigated by prominent Socialist Party politician Ségolène Royal, who allegedly threatened to withdraw public subsidies for the event if the artist was allowed to perform. This sparked a critical reaction from President Nicolas Sarkozy, who accused Royal of 'attacking freedom of expression'. (BBC, Freemuse)

Germany

In April 2010, authorities blacklisted 11 Jamaican dancehall albums released between 2008 and 2011. Among those singled out for anti-homosexual and violent lyrics were prominent stars **Sizzla**, **Elephant Man**, **Bounty Killer**, **Capleton**, **TOK** and **Baby Cham**. The list, compiled by the German Federal Department for Media Harmful to Young Persons, makes it illegal for minors to purchase material produced by the blacklisted artists and prohibits any advertising promoting the music. (Freemuse, *Jamaica Observer*)

Grenada

The government denied performance work permits to popular Jamaican dancehall artist **Vybz Kartel** and his band, whose controversial lyrics were described as violent. Kartel was scheduled to perform his 'Rap-It-Up' concert in Grenville, St Andrews, on 2 May 2009 to mark the launch of the singer's condom range on the island. (Freemuse, *Jamaica Star*)

Guyana

The ban on Jamaican dancehall performer **David 'Mavado' Brooks** was lifted on 11 September 2009. The Ministry of Home Affairs barred Mavado in April 2008 on the grounds that he constituted a security threat because his lyrics celebrate gun culture and homophobia. Other Jamaican dancehall artists, including **Rodney 'Bounty Killer' Price,** were banned at the same time. Mavado performed in Guyana on 18 and 19 September. (Caribbean e-News, Freemuse)

India

The Bharatiya Janata Party in Haryana promised to ban western music if it was successful in the October 2009 regional elections. The Hindu nationalist party's manifesto stated that the ban would protect the 'ancient and rich Haryanvi culture'. Poll results on 22 October revealed that the party did not gain enough votes to play a role in the state's assembly. (Freemuse, Rediff News, the *Straits Times*)

Indonesia

In March 2009, Buddhists put pressure on French entertainment chain **Bar Bhudda** to close its only branch in Asia. The protesters accuse the bar of blasphemy because it uses religious symbols as part of its decor. They have campaigned for the Jakarta bar to close since its opening in December 2008, praying and burning incense outside the premises. Pressure escalated during the second week of March when the religious affairs minister suggested that the company consider closure to encourage 'harmony among religions'. (Irrawaddy, *Jakarta Post*)

International

In April 2010, YouTube was reported to have deleted the video 'Born Free' by pop artist **MIA** because of its graphic violence. But on 28 April, news emerged that the video-sharing site had applied an age restriction on viewing the clip. Viewers' efforts to locate it, coupled with the site's staff in charge of monitoring content, made the video almost inaccessible. 'Born Free' depicts people dressed as soldiers attacking and killing red-haired people. MIA stated that her intention was to encourage debate. (BBC, *Guardian*, *Wired*)

Iran

On 16 July 2010, a group of women performed Sama, the ecstatic Sufi dance, for the first time at Tehran's prestigious Vahdat Hall. Members of the Sufi faith have come under criticism from the authorities for their mystical approach to Islam. The all female **Ava-ye Mehrabani** (the Call of Kindness) group performed on stage with 35 frame drum musicians. Solo female singing has been banned since 1979, though no official restrictions exist prohibiting female musicians performing in public. (al Arabiya)

The **teaching of music** in private schools was outlawed in June 2010 because it clashes with traditional Islamic values, according to Education Minister Ali Bagherzadeh. Although music tuition was already prohibited in the nation's public schools, the new law extended this to Iran's 16,000 private schools. As a consequence, 1.1m students will not be allowed to play instruments, including those associated with traditional Iranian music. (Bloomberg, Freemuse)

On 7 May 2010, police arrested **80 young men and women** for attending an illegal concert and wearing 'inappropriate outfits' following a tip-off to the moral security police. They were taken to a Tehran court and charged with 'lustful pleasure-seeking'. Alcohol and music equipment were also seized. (*Guardian*)

Iraq

After years of dormancy following the 2003 invasion, the **Iraqi National Symphony Orchestra** performed in Baghdad's Green Zone to an audience of 250 people on 22 May 2010. The orchestra's director and chief conductor Karim Wasfi plans performances throughout the country, followed by a tour in Europe and the United States in 2011. (Freemuse, National Public Radio, Reuters)

On 15 July 2009, Baghdad's National Theatre hosted one of **Iraq's first rap concerts**. Local artists Mr Passion, J-Fire and Nine-Z, collectively known as Danger Zone Killer, performed in the busy shopping district of Karrada, an area that has regularly been targeted by insurgents. Self-proclaimed as 'Iraqi rap royalty', Mr Passion began rapping in 2004 and considers his music to be an outlet to express views on the current political situation. (AFP, Freemuse)

Kuwait

After the government made **music classes** compulsory, an ultra-conservative MP threatened to use the constitution to call the prime minister to account in November 2009. Islamist MP Mohammad Hayef insisted that music defied Islam and would lead to more westernisation in the country. Under pressure from some hardline politicians, the government has placed restrictions on **musical performances**. (AFP)

Lebanon

In May 2010, Lebanese authorities banned **Eileen Khatchadourian's** music video 'Zartir Vortyag' because its content evoked the Armenian genocide. The video was said to have been blocked out of fear that the Turkish ambassador might be offended and that Turkish-Lebanese relations would suffer as a result. No explicit reference to Turkey is made in the video. (Asbarez, Freemuse)

Malawi

Music by popular singer **Lucius Banda** was banned by the Malawi Broadcasting Corporation (MBC) in January 2010. In an internal memo, staff at MBC were given a 'final warning' not to broadcast Banda's music. The prohibition relates to his album *15/15*, which is critical of the government and accuses President Bingu Wa Mutharika of offering key roles to officials because they are from the Lhomwe region. Banda is one of the country's most popular musicians and is a former member of parliament. (Africa News, Unfree Media)

Malaysia

The Ministry of Information, Communication and Culture banned Muslims from attending American hip hop group the **Black Eyed Peas**' concert on 25 September 2009 because it was sponsored by the Irish brewery Guinness. The group had previously performed in Malaysia in 2007 at a concert open to the public. (CBC News)

Mexico

Singer **Sergio 'El Shaka' Vega** was killed on 26 June 2010, only hours after he dismissed rumours of his own death on an entertainment website. Vega, well known for performing *narcocorridos*, songs that celebrate the lives of drug barons, is believed to have been shot several times by members of rival drug gangs while driving to a concert in Sinaloa state in the northwestern part of the country. His murder is the latest in a number of attacks against *narcocorridos* singers over the past three years. (BBC)

On 20 January 2010, the ruling National Action Party (PAN) proposed new laws that could result in three-year prison sentences for musicians singing about drug barons and trafficking, as in the popular *narcocorridos* genre. A PAN spokesperson said that the law was designed to prevent incitement to crime, not to restrict freedom of expression. (Freemuse, *Guardian*)

Latin Grammy-winning accordionists **Ramon Ayala** and **Lupe Tijerina** were amongst eight musicians arrested at a Christmas party in Cuernavaca on 11 December 2009. Police authorities seized US$280,700, 16 guns and 1,700 rounds of ammunition from the party, which they claimed was sponsored by a drug cartel. The incident was the first reported occasion where *narcocorridos* singers were arrested during a drug raid. Ayala spent 40 days under house arrest, until the attorney general investigated his links to organised crime, drug trafficking and money laundering. All charges were later dropped. (Freemuse, the *Monitor*)

Narcocorridos singer **Carlos Ocaranza**, popularly known as 'El Loco Elizalde', was shot and killed in August 2009 as he left a concert in Guadalajara in western Mexico. His agent was also killed. Ocaranza survived a previous attempt against his life in 2008. (*El Universal*, Guanabee.com)

Nepal

In July 2009, Nepal Television censored a music video used as an

179

advertisement on the grounds that it encouraged civil war. The video, which featured the voices of singers **Devi Gharti** and **Krishna Devkota**, depicted a Maoist leader in a positive light. (Freemuse, myrepublica.com)

Nigeria

The Kano State Censorship Board cancelled **Kanfest**, an annual music festival organised and funded by the French embassy in the northern part of the country, on 26 February 2010. The board informed the organisers two hours before the festival was due to begin at a cultural centre in Kano, citing failure to obtain permission as the reason for the closure. The event has been running for several years and permission from the board has never been required in the past. (carmenmccain.wordpress, Freemuse)

Popular Hausa singer **Ala**, also known as **Aminu Ladan Abubaka**r, was arrested on 4 July 2009, following the release of his song 'Hasbunallahu', which was banned by the Kano State Censorship Board. He was denied bail on 7 July 2009 and charged with failing to obtain permission from the board. He was released from prison on 9 July and given instructions not to speak with journalists. (Freemuse)

A Kano chief magistrate ruled it illegal to listen, sell and circulate 11 **Hausa songs** on 6 June 2009. Though authorities said the ban was introduced because the material was obscene, most of the proscribed songs are critical of the government and the censorship board. (carmenmccain.wordpress, Fileroom.org, Freemuse)

The commissioner for the environment closed the **New Afrika Shrine**, the Lagos club run by musician Femi Kuti and his sister Yeni Anikulapo Kuti, on 26 May 2009, following reports that the club was a 'nuisance' because it allowed street trading outside its premises. Femi

Kuti is an outspoken critic of the Nigerian government and corruption in Africa. The club carries on the legacy of his father Fela Kuti, who was jailed and physically harassed for criticising the government through his music. The club re-opened on 3 June. (Art's Own Kind, Freemuse, *Village Voice*)

Pakistan

Five people were injured and ten music stores damaged in a bomb attack on a **music and video market** in the town of Jand in the Punjab province on 28 January 2010. It is estimated that around 800 music stores in the northwestern part of the country were bombed between 2006 and 2009. Hundreds of musicians fled the Swat valley after the Pakistani government reached an agreement with the Taliban allowing Sharia law to be enforced in some parts of the North West Frontier Province. (CNN, Freemuse, Medialine News Agency, Pakistan Press Foundation)

On 15 December 2008, unidentified militants attacked two vehicles transporting popular Pashtun singer **Sardar Yousafzai** and members of his orchestra. Five musicians were injured, and a few days later, harmonium player **Anwar Gul** died from his injuries. Yousafzai was thought to be the target of the attack. (Freemuse)

Palestine

Two Palestinian artists were targeted separately in the An-Nafaq region of Gaza City in October 2009. On 14 October, **Salah al Qishawi** was attacked and required hospital treatment for his injuries. On 19 October, singer **Khalid Faraj** from the Baladna Music Band was abducted by armed men as he travelled home from a wedding party. His bandmates managed to follow the gunmen and later found Faraj with 39 separate injuries. (Freemuse)

Palestinian authorities banned Israeli Arab **Wafa Younes** from a West Bank refugee camp after a youth orchestra she conducted played for a group of Holocaust survivors in Israel in April 2009. The organiser of the event, charity director Kaynan Rabino, stated that the event's goal was 'to bring people's hearts closer together'. Leaflets distributed in the Jenin area of the West Bank accused Younes of exploiting children and warned Palestinians against any involvement in similar events in the future. (al Jazeera, Freemuse, *Guardian*, Reuters)

Poland

Adam Darski, who plays in Polish heavy metal band Behemoth under the pseudonym 'Nergal', was charged on 8 March 2010 for offending religious feelings. Darski faced a possible prison sentence for reportedly calling the Catholic Church 'the most murderous cult on the planet' and tore up a copy of the Bible on stage during a concert. The head of the All-Polish Committee for Defense Against Sects sued Darski for promoting Satanism. On 28 June 2010, the Behemoth website announced that the District Court of Gdynia had dismissed the case against Darski, stating that his actions had not been recognised as a crime. (Freemuse)

Russia

On 16 July 2009, the prosecutor's office in St Petersburg revealed that some **music fans** were under surveillance. Skinheads, anarchists and opposition groups were also said to be on the authorities' register, with some secret agents attending punk and death metal concerts. The classification of music fans as potential extremists was regarded by free expression advocates as further expansion of the government's extremism laws. In 2008, the band **Televizor** saw their performance on live television cancelled due to anti-government lyrics. Heads of radio and television stations are often employed by the state and refrain from broadcasting music that might offend the government. Those in charge of privately-owned stations are said to be wary of making controversial decisions out of fear of losing their licences. (*Guardian, St Petersburg Times*)

Rwanda

The International Criminal Tribunal for Rwanda upheld charges against singer **Simon Bikindi** on 18 March 2010. The Tanzanian-based tribunal convicted Bikindi, one of Rwanda's most prominent singers, of inciting racial hatred on 2 December 2008. The charges stem from an incident in 1994 when Bikindi addressed a crowd of ethnic Hutus, urging them to kill Tutsis. (BBC, Reuters)

St Lucia

The government announced that **Vybz Kartel** was banned from performing on the island on 20 April 2010. Authorities were concerned that the dancehall artist's performance, scheduled for 1 May, would see an increase in crime and anti-social behaviour. Civil society groups, women's rights campaigners and religious groups protested against plans to allow the singer's performance. Guyana, Grenada and Barbados had also banned his performances in previous weeks. (*Jamaica Observer*, St Lucia News Online)

Somalia

Radio stations stopped playing music on 13 April 2010 following an order issued on 3 April by Islamist insurgents, saying music broadcasts violated Islamic principles. Abdulahi Yasin Jama, head of programmes at Tusmo Radio, said that stations had no choice but to comply with the order. Only the government-controlled Radio Mogadishu, which is protected by African Union peacekeepers, and

the UN-funded Radio Bar-Kulan, based in Nairobi, resisted the order. (BBC, *New York Times*)

On 30 September 2009, **Radio Warsan** director **Hilal Sheik Shueyb** and news editor **Mohamed Aden Dhaysane** were arrested and the station shut down by al Shabaab forces. The privately-owned radio was targeted for playing songs in defiance of orders not to broadcast music or any 'un-Islamic' programming. (International Press Institute, NUSOJ)

Members of the Islamist armed group al Shabab raided **Radio Jubba** in Baidoa on 26 April 2009. The Islamist insurgents closed the station and arrested three of its journalists, **Muktar Mohamed Atosh, Mohamed Adawe Adan** and **Mohamed Nur Mohamed**, for not obeying orders. The journalists were freed on 29 April, and the station allowed back on air without music. (journalism.co.za, RSF)

South Africa

On 26 March 2010, a Johannesburg court prohibited the singing of a controversial anti-apartheid song, **'Ayesab'amagwala'** (The cowards are afraid) on the grounds that it incited violence against white farmers. On more than one occasion, African National Congress (ANC) youth leader Julius Malema sang the controversial lyrics 'shoot the Boer' to ignite already tense racial relations. After the murder of white supremacist leader Eugene Terreblanche on 3 April, Malema sang the lyrics again at a press conference on 8 April. The day before, the ANC appealed to its members not to sing the song. (BBC, Freemuse)

Syria

Seven men, including members of a **wedding music band**, were arrested at a Kurdish wedding on

3 October 2009. Accused of singing patriotic Kurdish songs, the musicians were taken to a prison in Qamishli along with members of the wedding party, where they were said to have been physically harassed. (Freemuse, Gilgamesh Center for Kurdish Studies and Research)

Turkey

Singer **Cevdet Bağca** was sentenced to 10 months' imprisonment on 4 July 2010 after urging his audience to remember three artists and a child killed by the country's security forces. He was convicted of 'sympathising with an illegal organisation' by a court thought to be comprised of secret police officers. (Bianet)

At a hearing at the beginning of May 2010, a public prosecutor ruled that Kurdish singer **Ferhat Tunç** could face imprisonment of up to 15 years for 'spreading propaganda'. The charges, brought under the country's anti-terrorism laws, were in response to a speech Tunç delivered on 15 August 2009 at a festival. Tunç has faced similar charges in the past and has also received death threats. (Freemuse, Kurdnet)

A criminal court in Diyarbakır handed down 10-month prison sentences to 13 members of the **Bahar Cultural Centre** (BKR) on 23 April 2010. The Kurdish musicians and artists were charged with 'violating the law on assembly and demonstrations' and told they were banned from performing or taking part in any artistic events for one year. **The BKR Music and Theatre Group** were prosecuted following their performances at a cultural festival as part of Kurdish new year celebrations. (Freemuse)

On 25 March 2010, Kurdish singer **Rojda Şenses** was sentenced to one year and eight months' imprisonment for instigating 'propaganda for a terrorist organisation' during concerts. Şenses testified in court in Istanbul on 11 February, defending

181

her performance of the song 'Heval Kamuran' in two separate concerts. The sentences were later reduced. (Freemuse, Voice of Kurdish-American Radio for Democracy, Peace and Freedom)

Emrah Gezer was killed outside a bar in Ankara in early 2010 after singing Kurdish songs during a night out with friends. A woman in the bar accused the revellers of belonging to the banned Kurdish Workers Party (PKK). In the initial trial on 11 February, two police officers, who had been sitting next to the woman who heckled the group, were charged with murder. She was charged with incitement to murder. (Freemuse, Human Rights Foundation Turkey)

Uganda

Two songs by musician **Mathias Walukagga** were banned from being performed, played or distributed on 3 November 2009. The songs, 'Bwino W'omutembeeyi' (The secrets of the hawker spilled) and 'Tuleppukke' (Well, let's deal with each other) allegedly libelled the owner of Samona Cosmetic Products, Ssalongo Kasawuli. The banning of the songs, and the subsequent arrest of Walukagga on defamation charges, were the culmination of a long-standing argument between Walukagga and Kasawuli. Prior to the case being lodged at court, the businessman commissioned another singer to release a song criticising Walukagga. (Freemuse, New Vision)

United Kingdom

On 12 April 2010, communications regulator Ofcom criticised radio DJ **Steve Penk** for joking on air about a woman's attempted suicide, and for playing Van Halen's 'Jump' during his morning programme. Several song requests, including 'Jumping Jumping' by Destiny's Child and the Van Halen song, were called in to the programme by listeners stuck in a traffic jam caused by the incident. Ofcom received 57 complaints over Penk's behaviour, deeming it offensive, insensitive and in violation of the broadcasting code. Penk refused to apologise for the decision, saying he was standing by his audience. (*Guardian*)

On 16 October 2009, the Metropolitan Police altered a performance licensing form that had come under criticism for racial bias. Form 696 originally included a question about the style of music to be performed at a planned event and required details of the 'make-up of patrons', both of which were criticised by music and equal rights groups. The new form stipulates that the police can retain data for up to six years. (*Guardian*)

Campaigners voiced concern over the impact of new visa regulations on artists and musicians hoping to perform in the country. Introduced in November 2008 to minimise illegal immigration, those affected include Russian dancers working for the Wales-based company **Ballet Russe**, who were all refused visas at the beginning of 2009, and the **Patiala Pipe Band** from Pakistan, who were due to travel to Scotland to take part in a pipe band championship over the weekend of 11–12 August 2009. The UK regulations were thought to be part of a European-wide tightening up of visa requirements. In June 2009, Zimbabwean band **Mookomba** was forced to cancel their European tour of nine countries, including the UK, due to their visas not being processed. (BBC, *Guardian*, *Sunday Times*)

The London performance by a group of 19-year-old Israeli soldiers-turned-singers was cancelled on 4 May 2009 because the owners of the theatre hall claimed it was 'political'. The organisers, the **Zionist Federation**, denied the claim and accused the theatre hall's owners of censorship. The five soldiers had been due to perform a medley of national songs at the Bloomsbury Theatre. (Freemuse)

United Kingdom/ United States of America

Britney Spears agreed to rename and re-record part of her song 'If U Seek Amy' on 20 January 2009 after some radio stations in the US and UK, including BBC's Radio 1, deemed it too offensive to play. The title of the song spelled out the word 'fuck', which is not allowed on the BBC and FM stations in the US. Some families in the US also called for the song to include a 'parental advisory' warning when sold in shops. (Freemuse, *Independent*)

Zimbabwe

The Zimbabwe Broadcasting Company banned the Sungura musician **Hosiah Chipanga**'s album *Hero Shoko* from being played on national radio on 21 June 2009. Head of programming for Radio Zimbabwe said the album was banned because it was overtly political, suggesting that it might be dangerous to play Chipanga's music at a time of 'national healing'. Corruption in President Mugabe's Zanu-PF party is among the topics addressed in Chipanga's album. Music by **Thomas Mapfumo** and **Leonard Zhakata** was also denied airplay on the station. (Freemuse, Zimbabwe Online Press)

Edited by Natasha Schmidt
Compiled by Ángel García Català, Ed Gillett, David Paton, Pete Ward and Kathie Wu
DOI: 10.1177/0306422010381330

FLOW THE FREE WORD ESTIVAL

"

4 SEP – 5 OCT 2010

XPLORING THE FLOW OF IDEAS

XEL SCHEFFLER / AS BYATT / DANIEL PENNAC

UENTIN BLAKE / ISMAIL KADARE / JOHN HEGLEY

UTH PADEL MAHSA VAHDAT / KNUT REIERSRUD

RICA WAGNER SAM LEITH / ELAINE FEINSTEIN

AKE ARNOTT / LOUISE STERN / ORLANDO GOUGH

AYU NAIDU / KATE FOX / NADEED ASLAM / BIDISHA

IMON MOLE / DOVEGREYREADER / NICHOLAS

HAKESPEARE /ROSS SUTHERLAND / JOE DUNTHORNE

HAZEA QURAISHI / AMARJIT CHANDAN

HYAM ALLAMI / SARAH ARDIZZONE

r more information visit www.freewordonline.com/flow,
ll 020 7324 2570 or drop into to Free Word Centre,
) Farringdon Road, London ECIR 3GA